Ruby For Kids

FOR DUMMIES®
A Wiley Brand

by Christopher Haupt

FOR DUMMIES®
A Wiley Brand

Ruby For Kids For Dummies®

Published by: **John Wiley & Sons, Inc.,** 111 River Street, Hoboken, NJ 07030-5774, www.wiley.com

Copyright © 2016 by John Wiley & Sons, Inc., Hoboken, New Jersey

Published simultaneously in Canada

For general information on our other products and services, please contact our Customer Care Department within the U.S. at 877-762-2974, outside the U.S. at 317-572-3993, or fax 317-572-4002. For technical support, please visit www.wiley.com/techsupport.

Wiley publishes in a variety of print and electronic formats and by print-on-demand. Some material included with standard print versions of this book may not be included in e-books or in print-on-demand. If this book refers to media such as a CD or DVD that is not included in the version you purchased, you may download this material at http://booksupport.wiley.com. For more information about Wiley products, visit www.wiley.com.

Library of Congress Control Number: 2015941961

ISBN 978-1-119-05590-7 (pbk); ISBN 978-1-119-05599-0 (ebk); ISBN 978-1-119-05600-3

Manufactured in the United States of America

10 9 8 7 6 5 4 3 2 1

Contents at a Glance

Table of Contents

Introduction

Ruby For Kids For Dummies is an introduction to the basics of coding using the Ruby programming language. In each chapter, I walk you through a step-by-step set of instructions to create a Ruby program for your Mac or Windows computer. You don't need to have any programming experience to understand this book, but you do need to have a sense of curiosity and adventure!

The Ruby programming language has been around since the mid-1990s and has become very popular with web application programmers. It can be used for so much more than just web apps. In this book, you'll see that you can use Ruby for small "command line" tools and calculations; larger programs for home, work, or school; or even graphical games (and I'll show you a lot of games).

Ruby was designed by its creator Yukihiro Matsumoto to be both fun and productive. My hope is that as you explore the projects in this book, you'll definitely have fun and be inspired to continue to use Ruby (or any other programming language) to realize your own coding ideas.

Programming in general is similar to sports, music, or even creative arts. It's hard to just absorb a book on the subject and expect to understand it completely or start to gain mastery of the topic. Instead, you need to have keyboard time and practice. Even professional coders continue to practice throughout their careers.

By exploring and playing around with the projects here, you'll be taking the first steps down a really interesting Ruby-colored road.

About This Book

Programming is a large topic, and Ruby itself is a very powerful language. I'll be working to shed light on some of the more fundamental parts of Ruby and coding in general. There is no rush to finish the projects in the book. Go through each *Ruby For Kids For Dummies* project as quickly or slowly as you like. Each chapter's project is a self-contained useful utility or fun game. Along the way, you'll learn how to use the very same tools that the professionals use, and learn the kinds of techniques that will help you grow as a programmer.

You don't need to have any previous programming experience, but if you know a little, that's fine — you'll pick up how Ruby does things and also see some similarities to other languages. I'll show you the "Ruby way" when applicable, but I'll also show the easy way when you're just learning the concepts.

Topics covered in this book include the following:

✔ The general way to structure simple Ruby programs

✔ Ruby expressions and operators

✔ Organizing functionality using methods and objects

✔ Basic ways to represent data like numbers, strings, and arrays

✔ Using loops

✔ Making choices with `if...else` statements

Learning to program with Ruby isn't just about writing code in the language. You also need to learn about the tools, resources, and community that stand behind the language.

Ruby has become so popular because it's a relatively simple language to learn, and the tools needed to write Ruby, test it, and run it are widely available and free. In this book, I help you get started with just a few basic, free, programs that do everything you need to create some pretty sophisticated pieces of software.

You'll also learn about general programming techniques, and most important, see a wide variety of projects that will pique your interest and hopefully encourage you to take your exploration to the next level.

To make this book easier to read, you'll want to keep in mind a few tips. First, all Ruby code and all terminal commands appear in monospaced type like this:

```
puts "hello programs! Welcome to Ruby"
```

The margins on a book page don't have the same room as your monitor likely does, so long lines of Ruby and any output it creates may break across multiple lines. Remember that your computer sees such lines as a single line of Ruby. I show that everything should be on one line by breaking it at a punctuation character or space and then indenting any overage, like so:

```
def room_type
["cave", "treasure room", "rock cavern", "tomb",
    "guard room", "lair"].sample
end
```

Ruby is case sensitive, which means that swapping the use of uppercase or lowercase letters or a combination of the two can break things. In order to make sure that you get the correct results from the projects in the book, always stick to the same capitalization and spelling that I use.

Ruby also cares about the kind of quotation marks that you use! So, if you see double quotes (") or single quotes ('), be sure to use what I show and make sure they're straight and not curly.

Foolish Assumptions

To understand programming, you need a bit of patience and the ability to think logically about a topic. You don't need to be a computer guru or a hacker. You don't need to be able to build a computer or take one apart (although that might be fun!). You don't need to know a bit from a byte or how many programmers it takes to screw in a new light bulb.

However, I do need to make some assumptions about you. I assume that you can turn your computer on, that you know how to use a mouse and a keyboard, and that you have a working Internet connection and web browser. You should also know how to find and launch programs on your computer.

In this book, I explain everything else you need to get set up and coding in Ruby.

Icons Used in This Book

Here's a list of the icons I use in this book to flag text and information that's especially noteworthy.

The Technical Stuff icon highlights technical details that you may or may not find interesting. Feel free to skip this information, but if you're the techie type, you might enjoy reading it.

The Tip icon highlights helpful tips that show you easy ways or shortcuts that will save you time or effort.

Whenever you see the Remember icon, pay close attention. You won't want to forget the information you're about to read — or, in some cases, I remind you about something that you've already learned that you may have forgotten.

Be careful. The Warning icon warns you of pitfalls to avoid.

Beyond the Book

I've put together a lot of extra content that you won't find in this book. Go online to find the following:

- **Cheat Sheet:** An online Cheat Sheet is available at www. dummies.com/cheatsheet/rubyforkids. Here, you find information on basic Ruby statements, conditions, loops and objects; a list of words that can't be used as Ruby variables or methods; a list of some of the useful methods provided by common Ruby classes; descriptions of common errors and what may cause them; and some small snippets of useful Ruby.

- **Web Extras:** Online articles covering additional topics are available at www.dummies.com/extras/rubyforkids. In these articles, I cover things like good ways to organize your Ruby class, some common Ruby shortcuts (also called "idiomatic Ruby"), Ruby troubleshooting tips, and more.

Where to Go from Here

Programming is a blast, and doubly awesome with Ruby. Even Ruby's creator wants you to have fun! After you learn the basics, you'll start to find all kinds of things you can do with your new-found powers.

I'm very interested to hear how it goes as you learn Ruby! If you want to show me your new ideas, bug fixes, or enhancements to my projects, or if you have programs you come up with on your own, you can do so on Facebook (www.facebook.com/mobirobo), on Twitter (www.twitter.com/mobirobo_inc), or via email at ruby@mobirobo.com.

Part I
The Most Basic Building Blocks

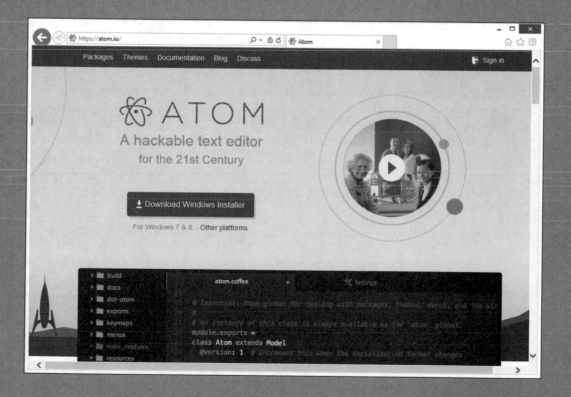

In this part . . .

For Dummies can help you get started with lots of subjects. Visit www.dummies.com to learn more and do more with *For Dummies!*

Getting Started with Ruby

Computers are almost everywhere today — from laptops, tablets, or phones, to TVs, watches, medical devices, kitchen appliances, cars, spaceships, big factories, little robots, and millions of other places large and small.

How do computers know what to do inside all these things? Someone has to teach them! Behind every cool animated movie, website, game, vehicle, or device, someone has worked hard to instruct a computer on how to perform its task. That person was a programmer.

In this chapter, I give you a little background about programming and how programmers organize their thoughts when writing computer software or code. I share some background about Ruby, the programming language I cover throughout this book. Then I tell you how to install the tools you'll use for all the projects in the rest of the book.

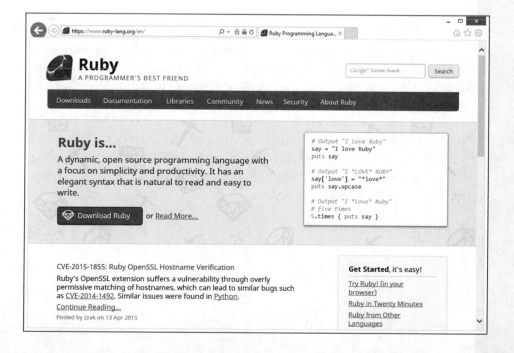

What Is Programming?

Computers are kind of dumb by themselves. Without a person to tell it exactly what to do, a computer will just sit there. Everything a computer does — and I mean everything, from the display of pictures and text on a screen, to the understanding of what you type on a keyboard or touch and swipe on a tablet — requires some software to interpret signals coming through the various circuits in one part of the computer and modify and send them to the right place in another part to get something done. That's a lot of work!

Fortunately, over the years, many smart people have come up with different ways to communicate clearly with computers. Writing instructions for a computer is called *programming* or *coding,* and the end result is a *program* or *software.*

A computer programming language shares many similarities to a human language. It has symbols and words (like nouns and verbs) that you put together following a *syntax* (rules for spelling, order, and punctuation).

When you start learning to program, you open up a wide world in which you can apply this knowledge when working with any technology that uses computers. You'll be able to read other people's programs to learn more about computers or to use code you write to solve homework problems, create puzzles, build a new game, create a website, or even control machines like robots.

Programs needs to be very precise in order to instruct a computer to do something. Imagine that you want to tell your friend to do something. For instance, how would you tell someone to sit down in a desk chair? You might say:

1. Pull the chair out.

2. Sit down.

Your friend is smart enough that your instructions make perfect sense, and she'll sit on the chair safely without falling over or anything crazy like that. People have a lot of knowledge they can use to interpret instructions like this.

Now, if you have to tell a computer to sit down, what would that be like? You have to be a *lot* more exact. For example, you would have to say:

1. Pull the chair away from the desk.

2. Walk around so your body is in front of the chair.

3. Turn around so your backside is facing the chair.

4. Make sure your body is exactly next to the chair.

5. Start bending your knees and lowering your body.

6. Keep bending your knees until your bottom makes contact with the seat of the chair.

7. Stop bending your knees when your weight is held by the chair.

Even these instructions might not be enough for a computer because they make some assumptions (like what your body parts are called).

Try it yourself: How would you tell a computer exactly how to do something like filling a glass with water?

Programmers need to think in this very detail-oriented way. As you learn to write computer programs, you'll get good at breaking a problem down into smaller and smaller parts. Each of those parts will eventually be a line of code that you create. Over time, you'll learn other techniques that help you identify the different objects you'll need to describe to the computer and the actions those objects will take. This will help you organize your code in ways that make it possible to create very sophisticated software. Pretty cool, huh?

Why Ruby?

There are many different computer programming languages out there. Each language has strengths and weaknesses. Some languages are easier if you're trying to control large machines. Some languages are specialized for mobile apps — the kind on an iPhone, for example. Some languages make it easy to create websites. And some languages are for doing science and engineering.

A general-purpose programming language is good for many different kinds of projects. There are many general-purpose programming languages to choose from. The important thing when you're wanting to learn programming is to pick something and dive into training yourself to think like a programmer. When you learn one programming language, learning another one is much, much easier.

In this book, I use the language Ruby. Ruby is a flexible, general-purpose language that is useful for many kinds of projects. It was created in the mid-1990s in Japan by Yukihiro Matsumoto (best known by his nickname, "Matz"). Don't worry — you don't have to learn Japanese to program with Ruby! Today Ruby is used around the world for all kinds of projects, by beginners and professionals alike.

Matz had a wonderful philosophy in mind when creating Ruby: He wanted programmers to be productive, enjoy programming, and be happy. This is one of my favorite things about Ruby: As you learn it and write programs, you'll have fun!

What Tools Do You Need?

Most obviously, you need a computer that's running a current version of a consumer desktop operating system (Mac OS X or Windows).

If you're using a computer with Linux on it, you can still follow along with the projects in this book. I won't be going through the instructions here. Instead, check out the official Ruby documentation: www.ruby-lang.org/en/documentation/installation. As long as your selected approach installs at least version 1.9.3 of Ruby, you should be okay.

For the projects in this book, you need only a few basic tools, and they're all free.

First, you need Ruby installed, as well as some other software that helps Ruby use the capabilities of your computer. I walk you through how to install Ruby in this section.

Second, you need a text editor that is specifically for coding. Word processors don't work well when coding, so you'll use a tool that is built for programmers. There are a number of good, free code editors out there, and I help you install one of them in this section. (You may use any other editing program you like as long as it's a code editor of some kind.)

If you're on Windows

To run Ruby on Windows, you have to install Ruby and several developer tools. The following instructions have been tested with Windows 8 and 8.1.

1. Go to http://rubyinstaller.org in your web browser.

2. Click the big red Download button.

   A list of RubyInstallers appears.

3. Click Ruby 2.2.2 near the top of the RubyInstallers list (see Figure 1-1).

   Do *not* click Ruby 2.2.2 (x64).

   An installer program downloads to your computer.

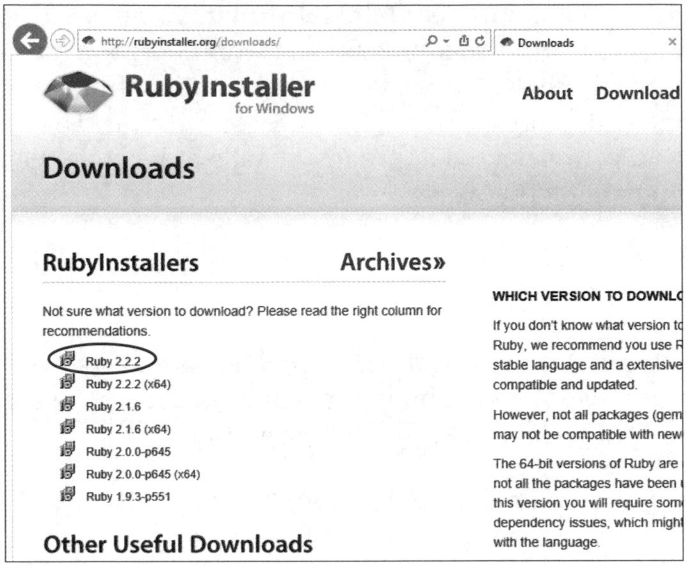

Figure 1-1: Click Ruby 2.2.2 to download installer.

4. Run the installer program by choosing Run Program (if Windows presents this option) or double-clicking the file when it's done downloading.

The installer will ask you to select a language to use during installation. Accept the license, and then the installer will have you set some configuration options. Leave the default folder choice alone, but *uncheck* the Install Tcl/Tk Support check box (you won't be using it for this book), and make sure that the other two check boxes — Add Ruby Executables to Your PATH and Associate .rb and .rbw Files with This Ruby Installation — are selected (see Figure 1-2).

When the installer is done, it will have created a topmost folder with all the Ruby software on your C: drive called C:\ Ruby22. You can use Windows 8 Desktop and the File Explorer to confirm that it's there (as shown in Figure 1-3).

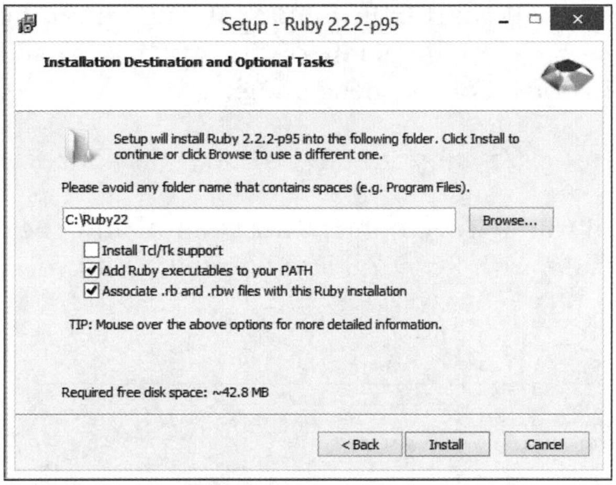

Figure 1-2: Setup Ruby installation settings.

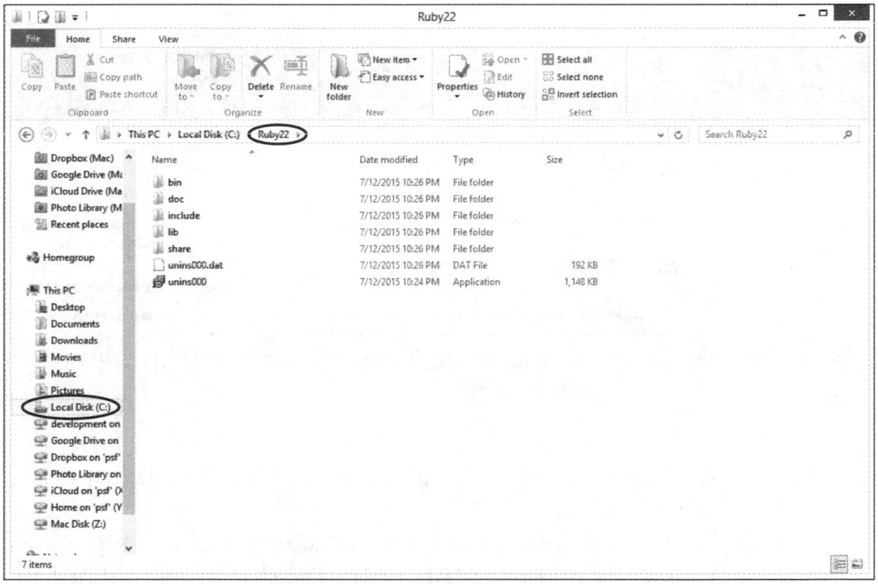

Figure 1-3: Confirm that the Ruby22 folder is created.

You must also download the Development Kit from `http://rubyinstaller.org` to get some of the cool tools used by the projects in this book. Follow these steps:

1. Go to the `http://rubyinstaller.org` in your web browser.

2. Scroll down to the Development Kit section and click the file under "For use with Ruby 2.0 and above (32bits version only)" (see Figure 1-4).

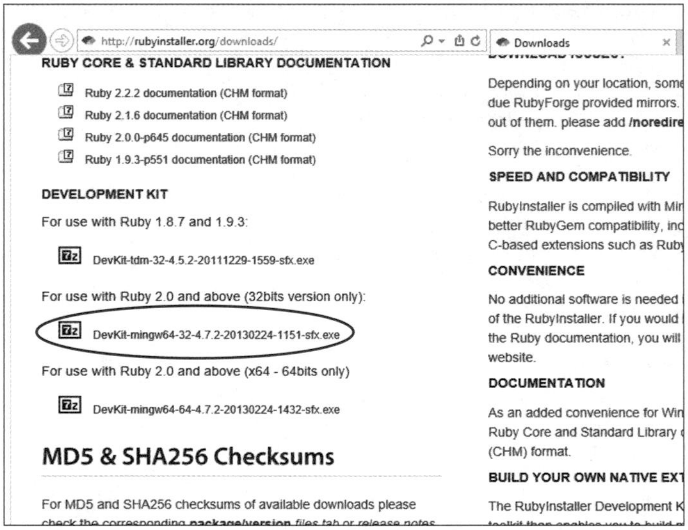

Figure 1-4: Download the Development Kit for Ruby 2.0 and above. Be sure to click the 32bits version.

An installer program downloads to your computer.

3. Run the Development Kit installer by choosing Run Program (if Windows presents this option) or double-clicking the file when it finishes downloading.

The installer will ask you where to put the kit. You want to put the kit in its own folder, not in the Ruby folder you selected in Step 1. To make things easy for the projects in this book, select a folder next to the `Ruby22` one at the top of your `C:` drive.

4. Enter **C:\DevKit** for the location, as shown in Figure 1-5.

Figure 1-5: Select the DevKit installation directory.

Now you need some final setup. Follow these steps:

1. Open your Windows launch screen (or use the Start Menu).

2. Click the Start Command Prompt with Ruby program (my machine looks like Figure 1-6).

Figure 1-6: Click Start Command Prompt with Ruby.

If you have a lot of programs installed in your launch screen, use the search feature and type **command** to help narrow down the choices.

In the command prompt application, you type commands to get things done. Typing commands is a low-level way of working with a computer. Before the mouse and graphical interface was invented, this was the only way to tell the computer what to do!

3. Change your location to the Developer Kit folder.

When you first open the command prompt application, you're usually in your home directory. To complete setup, you need to move to the DevKit directory. The display will show you a prompt that gives a hint of where you're starting from:

```
C:\Users\chris>
```

When you see commands in this book, you see them displayed next to the prompt. You don't need to type the prompt part, just the command line itself.

Change folders by typing **cd \DevKit** and pressing the Enter key to tell the computer you're done with that command.

You see the prompt change to your new location:

```
C:\Users\chris > cd \DevKit
C:\DevKit>
```

4. Use Ruby to set up more Ruby tools.

Development Kit has a Ruby setup program called dk.rb that you use for a couple of different steps. Enter the first command and watch for it to complete, as shown in Figure 1-7.

```
C:\DevKit> ruby dk.rb init
```

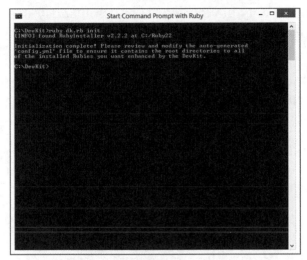

Figure 1-7: Initialize the Development Kit.

If you see the `Initialization complete!` message, Development Kit is ready to finish installing its tools.

5. Enter the install command and wait for it to complete (see Figure 1-8):

```
C:\DevKit> ruby dk.rb install
```

Figure 1-8: Install the Development Kit.

Phew! You only have to do these commands once to get your computer ready for Ruby programming and you're almost there!

6. The Development Kit is ready and now you can install Ruby gems (little add-on enhancements for Ruby) that you use for the more advanced projects in this book.

    You learn a lot more about Gosu, the graphics and game programming library in later chapters. Enter the command and review the progress messages (see Figure 1-9):

    ```
    C:\DevKit> gem install gosu
    ```

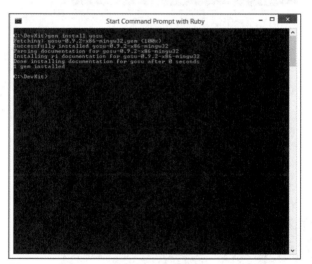

Figure 1-9: Install the Gosu gem.

You may get a Windows security warning saying that Ruby is trying to use the network. This is okay — you can select the default values in the dialog box. You may have to enter your password to dismiss the dialog box.

Wow, that was a lot, but now you have Ruby installed!

Now you will want a code editor to help make writing your programs easy:

1. In your browser, go to www.atom.io and click the Download Windows Installer button (see Figure 1-10).

Figure 1-10: Download the Atom Editor.

Atom is a free, powerful code editor that can be used for programming many different computer languages. It works well with Ruby.

An installer program downloads to your computer.

2. Run the Atom installer by choosing Run Program (if Windows presents this option) or double-clicking the installer program when it finishes downloading.

You see a progress dialog box. When the installer is done, the Atom editor starts up (see Figure 1-11).

You see the Atom welcome screen, which means you're all set to start programming with Ruby!

Figure 1-11: The Atom welcome screen.

Ruby is constantly being updated and improved. The projects in this book use the current release of Ruby at the time of the book's writing, version 2.2.2. Ruby uses a versioning scheme where the first number is the major version, the second number is the minor version, and the third number is the current build number (sometimes called the patch number). Most everything in this book should work with versions of Ruby all the way back to version 1.9.3, but it would be best if you use version 2.0.0 or better. On Windows, to utilize the game programming library Gosu, it's also important to select the version of Ruby and the Development Kit that indicate they are 32 bit.

If you're on Mac OS X

To install the needed developer tools for Mac OS X, you need to be logged in to your computer using an account with Admin access. If you're the only person using the computer, you're usually an administrator by default. If you share a computer at home, school, or work, you may need help to get access to an administrative account. You can check your access level by going to the Users & Groups control panel inside the System Preferences application (my machine looks like Figure 1-12). You only need Admin access during setup, not while completing the projects in this book.

Figure 1-12: Confirm that your account is an admin in Users & Groups.

To run Ruby on Mac OS X, you have to install Ruby and several developer tools. The following instructions have been tested on Mac OS X Yosemite (10.10.4). They should work fine with Mac OS X El Capitan (10.11.1) or Mavericks (10.9.5) as long as you're running the latest updates for that version of Mac OS X:

1. Open the `Applications` folder, and then open the `Utilities` folder (see Figure 1-13).

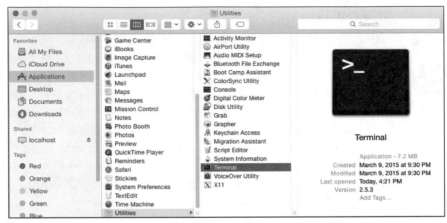

Figure 1-13: Locate the terminal program in the Utilities folder.

2. Open the terminal application.

You see a prompt indicator that looks like a dollar sign ($) (see Figure 1-14). In the terminal application, you type commands and press the Return key to get things done. Typing commands is a low-level way of working with a computer. Before the mouse and graphical interface was invented, this was the only way to tell the computer what to do!

Figure 1-14: The terminal application with a standard prompt.

Note that your default prompt will include information like the name of your computer, the directory you're in, and even who you're logged in as:

```
Christophers-MacBook-Pro:~ chaupt$
```

TIP

In this book, I omit the full prompt and just show the $ to save space.

3. Mac OS X comes with a version of Ruby preinstalled; check the version by typing **ruby –version** at the command prompt:

```
$ ruby --version
ruby 2.0.0p481 (2014-05-08 revision 45883)
    [universal.x86_64-darwin14]
```

In this example, the version of Ruby is 2.0.0, and the number following the letter p is the current patch or build number. On my machine, the patch level is 481. Although newer versions of Ruby are available, and the Mac's version will change if you install updates, the current version should work great for the projects in this book.

4. To use some of the Ruby gems (little add-on enhancements for Ruby) needed for the projects in this book, you must install Apple's command-line programming tools. These tools are a part of the free Xcode development tools package that Apple makes available. In the terminal, enter the following command:

```
$ xcode-select --install
```

After you press Return, the program will open a window to confirm you want to install the tools (see Figure 1-15).

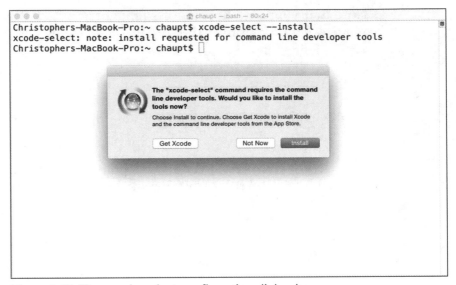

Figure 1-15: The xcode-select confirmation dialog box.

5. Click the Install button, agree to the license, and wait for the tools to get set up.

   This step will take a few minutes depending on the speed of your Internet connection.

6. Next, you install a set of software installation tools called Homebrew. Homebrew makes it easy to install and update additional software, called *packages*. Some of the projects in this book use Ruby gems that rely on low-level software to get their jobs done. Homebrew makes it much easier to get everything working. In your browser, go to the Homebrew web site, `www.brew.sh` (see Figure 1-16).

   You see instructions for installing Homebrew. The page shows a really long command that starts with `ruby -e`. You can copy it from the web page and paste it into your terminal window at the prompt.

Copy this entire command line.

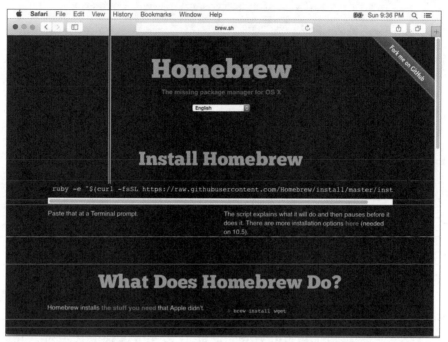

Figure 1-16: The Homebrew home page and installation command.

This is one long line, so if something goes wrong, make sure that you got the whole thing.

The command uses Ruby to install the Homebrew tool. It displays a warning about using sudo and then asks you for your password to finish the installation. This warning may be unfamiliar, but it's safe to proceed with the installation. Many progress messages will fly by on your screen (see Figure 1-17). If you get a message saying that you haven't agreed to the Xcode license, follow the instructions that are displayed and continue on here.

```
● ● ●                    ⌂ chaupt — bash — 80×24
or the deletion of important system files. Please double-check your
typing when using sudo. Type "man sudo" for more information.

To proceed, enter your password, or type Ctrl-C to abort.

Password:
==> /usr/bin/sudo /bin/chmod g+rwx /usr/local
==> /usr/bin/sudo /usr/bin/chgrp admin /usr/local
==> /usr/bin/sudo /bin/mkdir /Library/Caches/Homebrew
==> /usr/bin/sudo /bin/chmod g+rwx /Library/Caches/Homebrew
==> Downloading and installing Homebrew...
remote: Counting objects: 3660, done.
remote: Compressing objects: 100% (3491/3491), done.
remote: Total 3660 (delta 36), reused 651 (delta 28), pack-reused 0
Receiving objects: 100% (3660/3660), 2.97 MiB | 653.00 KiB/s, done.
Resolving deltas: 100% (36/36), done.
From https://github.com/Homebrew/homebrew
 * [new branch]      master      -> origin/master
Checking out files: 100% (3663/3663), done.
HEAD is now at af61c2c mapnik: update 3.0.0 bottle.
==> Installation successful!
==> Next steps
Run `brew help` to get started
Christophers-MacBook-Pro:~ chaupt$ ▌
```

Figure 1-17: Homebrew successfully completes installation.

If you're just learning about command-line programs on Mac OS X, you may be unfamiliar with using sudo. sudo is a way to give temporary permission to a program to use Administrator privileges. Homebrew needs this permission to set up the directories and software needed to do its job. The Homebrew installation program is used by thousands of people and is very careful about where it puts its software. If you ever need to use sudo yourself, you want to be extra careful that you type the associated commands correctly.

7. Once Homebrew installation is done, you can check that all is okay by typing the following command:

```
$ brew doctor
```

If everything is set up properly, you should see a message saying Your system is ready to brew. Otherwise, you may have some instructions to follow to finish updating Homebrew.

8. Homebrew's purpose is to make installing low-level software easier. Now, install some of the libraries of code you need for future projects:

   ```
   $ brew install sdl2 libogg libvorbis
   ```

   After you press Return, you see a series of progress reports as Homebrew installs the software (see Figure 1-18).

```
Christophers-MacBook-Pro:~ chaupt$ brew install sdl2 libogg libvorbis
==> Downloading https://homebrew.bintray.com/bottles/sdl2-2.0.3.yosemite.bottle
Already downloaded: /Library/Caches/Homebrew/sdl2-2.0.3.yosemite.bottle.1.tar.g
z
==> Pouring sdl2-2.0.3.yosemite.bottle.1.tar.gz
🍺 /usr/local/Cellar/sdl2/2.0.3: 75 files, 3.9M
==> Downloading https://homebrew.bintray.com/bottles/libogg-1.3.2.yosemite.bott
Already downloaded: /Library/Caches/Homebrew/libogg-1.3.2.yosemite.bottle.tar.g
z
==> Pouring libogg-1.3.2.yosemite.bottle.tar.gz
🍺 /usr/local/Cellar/libogg/1.3.2: 95 files, 672K
==> Downloading https://homebrew.bintray.com/bottles/libvorbis-1.3.5.yosemite.b
Already downloaded: /Library/Caches/Homebrew/libvorbis-1.3.5.yosemite.bottle.ta
r.gz
==> Pouring libvorbis-1.3.5.yosemite.bottle.tar.gz
🍺 /usr/local/Cellar/libvorbis/1.3.5: 155 files, 2.6M
Christophers-MacBook-Pro:~ chaupt$
```

Figure 1-18: Homebrew installs the necessary libraries.

9. Now you can install the Gosu gem that you use to build the projects later in this book. Enter the following command:

   ```
   $ sudo gem install gosu
   ```

   Ruby installs the gem and should provide a confirmation message (as shown in Figure 1-19).

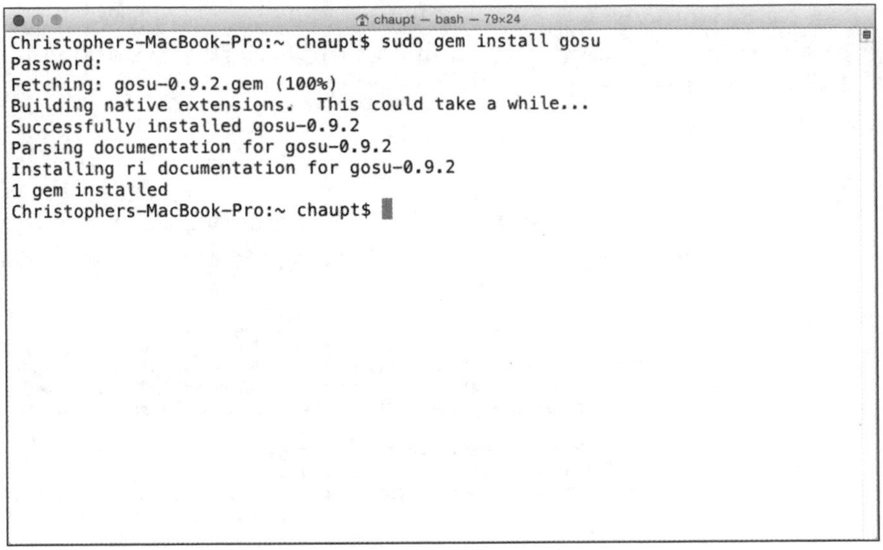

Figure 1-19: Gem installation completes successfully.

You need to use `sudo` here because when you install a Ruby gem, you install it for the entire system to use. Remember to take care when entering the command — you're giving it special permissions using the `sudo` program.

You have Ruby and its associated developer software ready to go, so now you need a programming editor:

1. In your browser, go to `www.atom.io`.

2. Click the Download for Mac button (see Figure 1-20).

   Atom is a free, powerful code editor that can be used for programming many different computer languages. It works well with Ruby.

   Depending on the settings of your browser, the Atom download archive may automatically uncompress or a zip file may be placed in your `Downloads` folder.

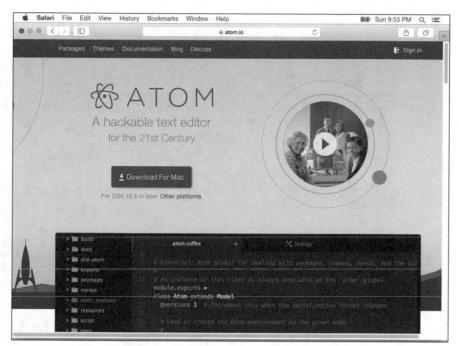

Figure 1-20: The Atom editor for Macintosh home page.

3. Drag the Atom icon to your `Applications` folder.

   If you see a zip file rather than the Atom icon, double-click the zip file to uncompress it manually.

4. Double-click the Atom icon in the `Applications` folder and check out the editor.

   You should see the Atom welcome screen (shown in Figure 1-21). You're all set to start programming with Ruby!

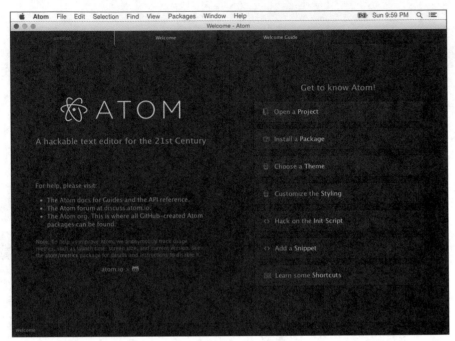

Figure 1-21: The Atom editor for Macintosh welcome screen.

Big Numbers

When you installed Ruby, a number of tools were placed on your computer. You'll use many of these tools time and time again as you learn to program. In this project, I show you how you can use a combination of your terminal program and Interactive Ruby to do quick experiments that let you try new things with Ruby.

You'll start at the very beginning and explore some of the most basic things you might ask a computer to do by exploring numbers, simple math, and storing results in the computer's memory using variables.

You probably didn't think Ruby could be used as a calculator for gigantic numbers, did you?

```
project02 — ruby — 86×27
irb(main):005:0> googol = 10**100
=> 10000000000000000000000000000000000000000000000000000000000000000000000000000000
000000000000000000000
irb(main):006:0> 20000000000 * 300000000 + 2
=> 6000000000000000000002
irb(main):007:0>
```

Starting Interactive Ruby

This project is completed entirely within your terminal (or console) program and uses Interactive Ruby (known as IRB or irb).

In this book, I refer to the language Ruby with an initial capital letter (as a name) and lowercase `ruby` to mean the Ruby command. Likewise, I use IRB to mean the name of the program, and `irb` to mean the command.

To get ready for this project, locate your terminal program (on the Mac) or the console with Ruby shortcut (on Windows). When that's running, everything else is the same.

I use the term *terminal* to mean the terminal or console program, whether on Mac or Windows.

At the command prompt, enter the `irb` command and press Return (Mac) or Enter (Windows):

```
$ irb
```

or

```
C:/> irb
```

if on Windows.

You now see the `irb` prompt:

```
$ irb
2.2.2 :001 >
```

Depending on your version of Ruby, the prompt may appear slightly different. In mine, it shows the current version of Ruby (`2.2.2`) and the current number of commands I've typed (when you first start IRB, you start on command `001`). When I show you commands in IRB in this book, my version and count may be different from yours, but that's okay.

Now IRB is ready for your commands, but before you start, let me show you how to leave IRB. The easiest way is to type **exit** and press Return (Enter). Alternatively, you can press Ctrl+D. You pop right out of IRB back to your terminal's prompt.

Go back into IRB and proceed to the next section.

Creating a development folder

Even though you won't be saving any files in this project, I recommend setting up a space on your hard drive for your work to be stored. Programmers call these spaces *directories,* but you may refer to them as folders. In this book, I use the two terms interchangeably.

In each project in this book, I describe how to initially set up your directories and files. The process is fairly similar for both Mac and Windows. I show you the commands to use in your terminal program.

First, I suggest you create a development directory to hold all your projects:

```
$ mkdir development
```

The new development directory will be created in your current directory. Remember that your prompt will look different on Windows and will normally display the current directory. Then inside of that, create a directory for that chapter's project:

```
$ cd development
$ mkdir project02
$ cd project02
```

Here, I changed the location to be within the development directory, made a new project directory (named project02 because you're reading Project 2's chapter), and then moved into that directory.

(continued)

(continued)

> **Remember:** If you get lost, you can navigate back to the top of your folders by using the `cd` command by itself and then changing directories again:
>
> ```
> $ cd
> ```
>
> You may also want to use the following command to move *up* one level to the parent folder of the current directory:
>
> ```
> $ cd ..
> ```

Entering Numbers

When you've started IRB, Ruby is waiting for something to do. I'll make this super simple.

Type the number **1** and press Return (Enter).

```
2.2.2 :001> 1
=> 1
2.2.2 :002 >
```

What did Ruby do? It showed you that it was listening by printing out number 1 again. The `=>` prompt is Ruby's signal that it's displaying some kind of result. After it's done, Ruby shows you a new prompt and waits for your next command. In future examples, I won't show you the next prompt, but you'll always see it on your screen!

Try entering a few more numbers, and you'll see Ruby keeps echoing your typing. Okay, this gets boring quickly, so let's move on.

Doing Some Basic Math

Ruby includes a large and powerful set of built-in capabilities. You use many of these capabilities as you progress through this book. One of the most basic is the capability to do simple arithmetic.

Enter **2 + 2** at the `irb` prompt and press Return (Enter):

```
2.2.2 :010 > 2 + 2
 => 4
```

Wow, Ruby can do math you learned in kindergarten! Let's look at the other arithmetic operations of multiplication, division, and subtraction:

```
2.2.2 :011 > 10 * 5
 => 50
2.2.2 :012 > 10 / 5
 => 2
2.2.2 :013 > 10 - 5
 => 5
```

Here, the symbols are a little different, but you get the results you'd expect. What if you want to try something even more complicated, like writing the math formula to convert degrees Fahrenheit to Celsius:

```
2.2.2 :018 > (212 - 32) * 5 / 9
 => 100
```

You're converting 212 degrees Fahrenheit by first subtracting 32, and then multiplying the result by $\frac{5}{9}$. Ruby does the math and displays the result, 100 degrees Celsius, which is correct.

Why did I include the parentheses in the formula? Try it again without them. Go ahead, I'll wait.

Did Ruby still give you the right answer?

No, because Ruby, like some other programming languages, processes lines of code in a certain order. In the case of mathematics, as well as other operations it can do, Ruby has a sense of priorities in terms of what order it will run the code. The parentheses provide a programming hint to do the math in the order you want it to be done.

Without the parentheses, Ruby runs the formula in the order of doing multiplication and division before addition and subtraction, which is very different from what you want. It's as if Ruby thought you said:

```
2.2.2 :020 > 212 - (32 * 5 / 9)
 => 195
```

 Programmers call this prioritization *order of operations* or *precedence,* a fancy term, indeed. If you find that lines of code aren't working the way you thought they would, check the precedence of the code you're using.

Supersizing the Math with Huge Numbers

Unlike a pocket calculator, or even the calculator on a smartphone, Ruby has amazing support for some truly gigantic numbers. Give this a try:

```
2.2.2 :022 > 1234567890 * 9876543210 *
    1234567899876543234567890
 => 15053411231914737792266671034604153889124 1000
```

There are 45 digits in that number! You can use the exponent operator (**) to raise a number by a certain power:

```
2.2.2 :026 > 10**2
 => 100
```

Try coming up with some really big numbers of your own and do some arithmetic on them.

If you haven't learned about exponents yet, all you need to know for this chapter is that it's the same as taking a number and multiplying it by itself the number of times indicated by the exponent number. So `10**2` means multiply 10 by itself two times: `10 * 10`. Sometimes you hear someone talking about exponents using the phrase some number *raised to a certain power*. In this example, 10 is raised to the second power.

Adding Memory by Storing Results in Variables

So far, you've just typed in some math formulas (or expressions) and immediately seen the results. This is fine for really short tasks, and it uses you, the human, to remember results and enter them again when needed.

But computers give you not only the power to calculate, but also the ability to store information for later retrieval.

You use variables to name a piece of memory, store information in that memory, and at some later time, retrieve the information again.

Programmers usually use the word *data* to refer to any information they're working on. I use that term in this book, too.

In Ruby, you typically name variables using lowercase letters, numbers, and underscores (_). Ruby expects a variable to start with a lowercase letter, and then you can use any combination of other lowercase letters, numbers, or the underscore. Ruby convention is to use "snakecase" when naming a variable. Snakecase splits up words with an underscore, kind of like using a blank space between words in an English sentence.

Here are some examples of variables:

```
hello_world_title
programmer1
blue_eyed_cat_name
b
a2
```

The last two examples, b and a2, are perfectly valid but what they're used for is a little mysterious. I suggest you use variable names that are meaningful to you. In this book, I use some very full names when the meaning needs to be clear, and I use some short names when appropriate.

In later projects, I describe other symbols and conventions for naming variables. The basic naming I explain here works for local variables. You'll use some additional symbols for other purposes later on.

To store data in a variable in Ruby, you "assign" the data to a variable using an equal sign (=):

```
2.2.2 :029 > age_of_my_dog = 4
  => 4
```

Unlike in math class, the equal sign here doesn't mean that the left side is equivalent to the right side (there is another symbol you'll see later that is used for that purpose). Instead, think of that equal sign as meaning "move the data on the right into the memory named with the variable on the left."

To get the data back out of the variable, you just use the variable name as if you typed the data in directly:

```
2.2.2 :030 > age_of_my_dog * 7
  => 28
```

You can assign the results of the calculation into a new variable:

```
2.2.2 :031 > dogs_age_in_people_years = age_of_my_
    dog * 7
 => 28
```

Ruby is pretty generous with respect to what you can name your variables. Almost anything goes. One of the few rules is that the name must not conflict with any of Ruby's built-in names for its commands. See the following for a list. If you do this accidentally, you get a syntax error, which I explain in the next section.

BEGIN	do	next	then
END	else	nil	true
alias	elsif	not	undef
and	end	or	unless
begin	ensure	redo	until
break	false	rescue	when
case	for	retry	while
class	if	return	while
def	in	self	__FILE__
defined?	module	super	__LINE__

Using Variables to Repeat a Calculation

I want to revisit our temperature conversion formula from the preceding section. Written with a variable f for Fahrenheit. The formula was as follows:

```
c = (f - 32) * 5 / 9
```

I'm going to assign f to be the degrees Fahrenheit I want to convert into Celsius:

```
2.2.2 :043 > f = 212
 => 212
```

```
2.2.2 :044 > c = (f - 32) * 5 / 9
 => 100
2.2.2 :045 > f = 100
 => 100
2.2.2 :046 > c = (f - 32) * 5 / 9
 => 37
2.2.2 :047 > f = 32
 => 32
2.2.2 :048 > c = (f - 32) * 5 / 9
 => 0
```

The temperatures seem correct, so I'll assume Ruby is doing the math correctly.

Note that I used a little trick that is hard to see in a book, but that you should try on your computer: I didn't actually keep typing that formula after the first time I entered it. Instead, I used a feature of IRB that allows me to recall a previous command. If you use the up and down arrow keys when in IRB, IRB will display earlier (or later, respectively) commands. You can make small edits to the command using the left and right arrow keys to move around. You simply press your Return (Enter) key to run the command again. This can save a lot of typing.

Fixing Things When Something Goes Wrong

What happens when you try to get Ruby to display a googolplex?

A *googol* is a fun term that means 10 raised to the 100th power. A *googolplex* is 1 followed by googol (10^{100}) zeroes. Supposedly, American mathematician Edward Kasner's 9-year-old nephew, Milton Sirotta, coined the term and defined it to be the digit "one, followed by writing zeroes until you get tired."

In IRB, store a googol in a variable called `googol`:

```
2.2.2 :030 > googol = 10**100
 => 1000000000000000000000000000000000000000000000000
    0000000000000000000000000000000000000000000000000
    00000
```

Now try raising 10 by a googol:

```
2.2.2 :031 > 10**googol
(irb):31: warning: in a**b, b may be too big
 => Infinity
```

I guess there are some limits to Ruby's math skills! Here, Ruby is showing you a warning that the command you just typed isn't working because part of the calculation is too big. It shows the results as `Infinity`, which seems about right to me.

Ruby tries to be helpful when some part of your program has a typo or does something unexpected. Ruby displays a warning or error message, often with information about where it found the problem in your code.

For instance, if I accidentally made a typo when doing some simple math, Ruby would tell me that I have a syntax error.

Syntax is like grammar in English. A programming language's syntax is the structure, order, and spelling of commands and statements in that language.

If I make an intentional spelling mistake:

```
2.2.2 :036 > 3j + 3
SyntaxError: (irb):36: syntax error, unexpected
    tIDENTIFIER, expecting end-of-input
3j + 3
   ^
    from /usr/bin/irb:11:in '<main>'
```

I didn't mean to type the letter j after the number 3, and unlike what you may write in school when learning algebra, this syntax is not valid Ruby.

Ruby displays an error message that's a little cryptic, but if you see syntax error and a line number or location, it gives you a place to start investigating what went wrong. In this case, Ruby helpfully displayed my incorrect line with a little arrow symbol pointing at the point it thought was wrong. Thank you, Ruby!

Let's see if Ruby can find another problem for us:

```
2.2.2 :037 > x + 5
NameError: undefined local variable or method 'x'
    for main:Object
    from (irb):37
    from /usr/bin/irb:11:in '<main>'
```

In this case, I tried to use a variable that I haven't stored anything in. Ruby doesn't know what to do here, because it can't find a variable named x (yet). You often see this error if you make a typo in the name of a variable (or method, which you'll learn about in a future project). Check your spelling and try again.

Another common Ruby error can be seen with this code:

```
2.2.2 :038 > x = nil
 => nil
2.2.2 :039 > x + 5
NoMethodError: undefined method '+' for nil:NilClass
    from (irb):39
    from /usr/bin/irb:11:in '<main>'
```

I haven't explained nil yet, but for now you can think of it as Ruby's way of representing "nothing." The error Ruby is showing us means that it doesn't know how to do addition with nil, which seems reasonable. In your code, this probably would mean you expected to receive results from some other part of the program, but the code returned nothing.

One last problem you occasionally see is if you try to do something with incompatible data:

```
2.2.2 :040 > x = "a"
 => "a"
2.2.2 :041 > x + 5
TypeError: no implicit conversion of Fixnum into
    String
    from (irb):41:in '+'
    from (irb):41
    from /usr/bin/irb:11:in '<main>'
```

I assigned the letter a to variable x. You learn more about strings and letters in the next project. Here, though, I tried to add the number 5 to the letter a. Clearly this is nonsense. Ruby thinks so, too, and tells me that it can't convert the data in a way to make it work.

Over the course of this book, you'll probably run into syntax errors the most often, because typos are the easiest bugs to make. When you see an error message, your best course of action is to carefully compare what you typed with the project's code.

Trying Some Experiments

In this project, you've seen some basic Ruby and how to use IRB to test out Ruby. You got to play with how Ruby can do math and how variables can help you store and recall data. Believe it or not, these are the fundamental building blocks on which modern programming is based. I explain a lot more in the coming projects, but manipulating data (numbers and arithmetic here), and storing and retrieving results, is what computers do all the time.

Take a few moments and try a few of these additional experiments:

- Use variables to store all the ages for your family or friends. Now add them together. What is the total age of everyone?

- Use Ruby to calculate the circumference of the Earth. The formula for circumference is 2 * PI * r. Pi is a special value used in geometry and other areas of math and science. Ruby provides this value to you automatically using a *constant* (a special variable whose value is locked down and can't be changed). You can access this value in IRB by typing **Math::PI**. To complete this experiment, you need to look up the value of r, which is the radius of the Earth.

- What is your age raised by the power of 10?

- What is the total if you add the first ten counting numbers (1, 2, 3, and so on up to 10)?

- Can Ruby store negative numbers? What about decimals? Try some math problems to confirm this.

- Try changing the temperature calculation to convert degrees Celsius to Fahrenheit.

Bigger Hello World

In this project, you start to work with letters and words.
Programmers often use the term *character* for a single letter and
the term *string* to mean one or more characters connected
together to form words or other patterns.

In this project, you again use Interactive Ruby (IRB) to learn
how to manipulate strings in Ruby and how strings are different
from numbers. You'll find out that there are some surprising
similarities, too, as you build a program to create a big HELLO!

```
project03 — ruby — 86×27
irb(main):029:0> 0.upto(6) do |count|
irb(main):030:1*   puts "#{h[count]} #{e[count]} #{l[count]} #{l[count]} #{o[count]}"
irb(main):031:1> end
H        H EEEEEEEEE L          L              000
H        H E          L          L            0    0
H        H E          L          L           0      0
HHHHHHHHH EEEEEEEEE L          L           0      0
H        H E          L          L           0      0
H        H E          L          L            0    0
H        H EEEEEEEEE LLLLLLLLL LLLLLLLLL     000
=> 0
irb(main):032:0> ▊
```

Starting Interactive Ruby

This project will be completed entirely within your terminal program using IRB. Follow these steps:

1. Start your terminal program.

2. At the prompt, type **irb** to get Ruby ready for the project.

If you aren't sure how to start your terminal program or IRB, check out the beginning of Project 1.

Knowing How Letters and Words Differ from Numbers

Programming languages keep track of the different kinds of data that you may want to work with in a program. For each type of data, the language will often provide common and unique capabilities for manipulating that data.

In Ruby, numbers are a type of data. As you saw in Project 1, you can do a variety of things with numbers, including performing the common arithmetic operations on them.

Letters, also know as characters, are another type of data in Ruby. Ruby can work with individual characters or collections of characters (like words or sentences). Ruby, like many other programming languages, calls these collections *strings*.

Characters, and strings that contain characters, can represent more than the standard alphabet (A to Z). Characters can be any of the visible symbols on your keyboard, and many that aren't directly visible (including things like spaces, tabs, and other special symbols).

This can get confusing, because that means that the character "3" and the number 3 look exactly the same. How does Ruby tell them apart?

You may have noticed that I snuck in something in that last paragraph: quotation marks! Ruby remembers that I used quotation marks when it repeats its results:

```
2.2.2 :004 > "3"
 => "3"
2.2.2 :005 > 3
 => 3
```

In Ruby, if I want to refer to a string of characters, no matter what they are, I put them between quotation marks. If I mean an actual number, I just write the digits of that number without quotation marks. Try this:

```
2.2.2 :001 > "hello"
 => "hello"
2.2.2 :002 > "1000"
 => "1000"
2.2.2 :003 > 1000
 => 1000
```

The first item, `"hello"`, is a regular English word and is a string. The second item, `"1000"`, is a string representing one thousand. And the third item, `1000`, is an actual number.

Behind the scenes, Ruby tracks the differences between these resulting objects and enables different kinds of powerful features depending on the type of that data.

In our programs, we use *straight quotes* (" "), and if you're using IRB or a programming editor like Atom, you should be okay. If you get an error when using strings, you may be using *typographic quotes,* also known as *curly quotes* (" "). This may be because you used a word processor (like Microsoft Word) to write code instead, and Ruby may get confused.

Going forward, I often use the word *object* to refer to a particular piece of data (like a number or string) and that data's different behaviors or features. Later, you'll learn about more complicated kinds of objects that allow you to build some really powerful programs.

Doing Math with Words

In Project 2, you learned how to do basic arithmetic with number data. It turns out that strings (and individual characters) have many built-in abilities, some of which look similar to symbols that look like arithmetic.

You can add two strings, and Ruby smashes the two strings together:

```
2.2.2 :006 > "hello" + "chris"
 => "hellochris"
```

Ruby isn't smart enough to put a space between the greeting and your name, but you can do that manually:

```
2.2.2 :007 > "hello " + "again chris"
 => "hello again chris"
```

Programmers call adding two strings together *concatenation* (or sometimes just *catenation*).

If you want to display a really excited welcome, you can use multiplication, and the string will be repeated the number of times you specify, like this:

```
2.2.2 :014 > "hello " * 5
 => "hello hello hello hello hello "
```

Note that you can't combine strings and numbers, so attempting to use the addition operator like the following leads to an error:

```
2.2.2 :015 > "hello number " + 5
TypeError: no implicit conversion of Fixnum into
    String
    from (irb):15:in `+'
    from (irb):15
    from /Users/chaupt/.rvm/rubies/ruby-2.2.2/bin/
    irb:11:in `<main>'
```

Now that we know Ruby tracks types of data, this error starts to be a little more meaningful in that it's called a `TypeError`, and it can't convert data automatically.

If you aren't sure about error messages in IRB or elsewhere in Ruby, see Project 1 for some hints about what the errors may mean.

Doing Other Things with Strings

Besides mathlike operations, strings have many other useful functions built in. As you get more familiar with programming, there will be times you want to do something more complicated, and Ruby will be there to save the day! I'll show you a couple examples in this section.

Imagine you needed to make your greeting appear to shout. In text, you may want to use all capital letters. But what if the variable doesn't already have a name in capitals? You can use a string function to solve that problem:

```
2.2.2 :031 > "Chris".upcase
 => "CHRIS"
2.2.2 :032 > name = "Chris"
 => "Chris"
```

```
2.2.2 :033 > name
=> "Chris"
2.2.2 :034 > name.upcase
 => "CHRIS"
```

To use an object's capabilities in Ruby, you follow the object with a period (also known as a *dot*) and then the name of the function you want to use. This technique works directly with an object like the string example above, or with a variable.

Here you're trying to use the upcase function to convert the string to capital letters on the fly.

In Ruby, an object's programmed capabilities or functions are known as *methods*. When you write code that makes an object use a method, you're "sending a message" to that object. I continue to use the terms *method* and *messages* in this book.

Try this example:

```
2.2.2 :035 > greeting = "hello there"
 => "hello there"
2.2.2 :036 > greeting.capitalize
 => "Hello there"
```

If you forgot to capitalize the greeting (or perhaps weren't sure if it was capitalized because you got the variable from somewhere else), you can use the string object's capitalize method to get the job done.

The official Ruby documentation site can be a little scary when getting started. For now, know that it's there and it's free. There are also lots and lots of free resources on the web that will help you expand your learning beyond this book. The Ruby String (www.ruby-doc.org/core-2.2.2/String.html) reference is just a small part of the available documentation. If you scan over the page, even if you don't understand it all, you'll see a huge number of methods that you can use in the future.

Storing Strings in Variables

Ruby lets you store any data type in a variable, and strings are no exception.

Here's how to store your name in a variable:

```
2.2.2 :016 > name = "Chris"
 => "Chris"
```

To confirm it's in there, do the following:

```
2.2.2 :017 > name
 => "Chris"
```

Create another variable for a greeting:

```
2.2.2 :018 > greeting = "Howdy there!"
 => "Howdy there!"
```

Now use string addition to assemble a full welcome message:

```
2.2.2 :019 > greeting + " " + name
 => "Howdy there! Chris"
```

See how I actually added three things together? I used my `greeting` variable, plus a string with a space in it, plus my `name` variable. You can string together as many strings as you want this way.

Try changing the order or adding together other words. You can also combine techniques to get more interesting results:

```
2.2.2 :024 > greeting = "hi "
 => "hi "
2.2.2 :025 > (greeting * 5) + name
 => "hi hi hi hi hi Chris"
```

Making Some Big Letters

Now that you've experienced the basics of strings, I'll walk you through creating some super-sized letters to print out a large "Hello" message.

I'm going to do this by building each letter from a combination of strings that, when printed out, form the shapes of a large letter. What does that mean?

Here's an example. Create four variables and carefully enter the strings for each. Note that each string is seven characters long when you count out the empty spaces.

```
2.2.2 :001 > a1 = "   A   "
 => "   A   "
2.2.2 :002 > a2 = "  A A  "
 => "  A A  "
2.2.2 :003 > a3 = " AAAAA "
 => " AAAAA "
2.2.2 :004 > a4 = "A     A"
 => "A     A"
```

Programmers call empty spaces created by pressing the spacebar or tab key on your keyboard *whitespace*. When such characters are printed out on paper, nothing is displayed in that spot and you just see the white color of the paper show through.

If you squint your eyes, you can sort of see the letter A. What happens if you concatenate the strings together?

```
2.2.2 :006 > a1 + a2 + a3 + a4
 => "   A     A A  AAAAA A     A"
```

Nope, that isn't it. Now it's just a long, strange collection of A's. You need to make each string print out on its own line, one on top of the other.

Ruby gives you a special character that means "go to the next line" (also known as new line or carriage return). To do this, you use the string `"\n"`.

You can do this manually:

```
2.2.2 :007 > a1 + "\n" + a2 + "\n" + a3 + "\n" + a4
 => "   A    \n  A A  \n AAAAA \nA      A"
```

But that isn't any better? What's going on?

Ruby is showing the results of a combined string, but it isn't really displaying it the way you want. To get Ruby to actually interpret the special symbols, you need to use a new Ruby command called `puts` (short for *put string*). Put the string in a variable and use `puts` to print it out:

```
2.2.2 :009 > big_a = a1 + "\n" + a2 + "\n" + a3 +
    "\n" + a4
 => "   A    \n  A A  \n AAAAA \nA      A"
2.2.2 :010 > puts big_a
   A
  A A
 AAAAA
A      A
 => nil
```

Success! That looks much better. Before I move on to creating the letters we need, let me show you a couple of ways to use Ruby to make programming with strings easier.

An easy way to combine words

You can add together your variables and new line symbols as you did above, but Ruby has a number of shortcuts for merging strings.

The first is called by a really fancy term: *string interpolation*. Don't worry about that for now — just check out how you combine strings:

```
2.2.2 :011 > big_a = "#{a1}\n#{a2}\n#{a3}\n#{a4}"
 => "    A    \n  A A  \n AAAAA \nA       A"
2.2.2 :012 > puts big_a
     A
    A A
   AAAAA
  A      A
 => nil
```

Instead of using the addition operator, you create one big string with double quotes, and use #{ } inside that string. That special combination of symbols means that any variable inside the curly brackets will have its value put in that location of the string.

In this example, you took the variables a1, a2, a3, and a4 and had their values automatically placed inside the new string. Because you included the newline character, too, the resulting string ends up being exactly like the longer sequence of addition operators you used.

Why use the string interpolation approach? Mainly, because it saves typing. You'll see it all the time as you read other Ruby code. In this book, I use it almost all the time when you need to combine data within a string.

An advanced way to combine strings together

But wait, there is always another way to do things in Ruby. Ruby has a type of data called an *array*. I'll share more about arrays in later projects. For now, think of an array like a special storage box with multiple compartments. You can put a different object in each compartment and separately retrieve those objects.

After numbers and strings, arrays are perhaps one of the most common data types you'll encounter when programming. You'll use arrays in almost all the future projects in this book.

Ruby represents arrays using square brackets like this:

```
2.2.2 :013 > big_a_array = [a1, a2, a3, a4]
 => ["   A   ", "  A A  ", " AAAAA ", "A     A"]
```

In this example, you assign the array to a new variable called big_a_array and put the separate a1, a2, a3, and a4 variables into the array.

The cool thing is that if you print out the array with puts, Ruby does the right thing automatically:

```
2.2.2 :014 > puts big_a_array
   A
  A A
 AAAAA
A     A
 => nil
```

This technique saves even more typing!

Now you have all the tools you need to display a big HELLO!

Creating the letter H

Start by creating the string parts for the big letter H:

1. Create the first h1 variable. This time, use nine characters for the total size of the string. In this step, there will be seven spaces between the two H's:

```
2.2.2 :015 > h1 = "H       H"
 => "H       H"
```

2. Create the h2 and h3 variables, which are identical to Step 1:

```
2.2.2 :017 > h2 = "H        H"
 => "H           H"
2.2.2 :018 > h3 = "H        H"
 => "H        H"
```

3. Check that any of your variables are the right size by using the string object's length method to print out its number of characters:

```
2.2.2 :019 > h3.length
 => 9
```

4. Create the h4 variable, which is the middle of the letter H:

```
2.2.2 :020 > h4 = "HHHHHHHHH"
 => "HHHHHHHHH"
```

Did you notice that you repeated yourself a lot for h2 and h3? The letter H is interesting because the top and bottom parts of the letter (at least for the capital version we're using) is the same.

Programmers say that the two parts of the letter are *symmetric*.

You can use the fact that the top and bottom are the same to save some work.

Programmers *love* to avoid typing! Look for patterns whenever you can and find ways to let your code do extra work for you.

5. Create h5 by assigning it the value of h1, because they look the same:

```
2.2.2 :021 > h5 = h1
 => "H           H"
```

6. Repeat Step 5 for variables h6 and h7:

```
2.2.2 :022 > h6 = h1
 => "H         H"
2.2.2 :023 > h7 = h1
 => "H         H"
```

7. Put all the parts of the letter into an array for storage and test it out. Use the variable named h to hold the array:

```
2.2.2 :024 > h = [h1,h2,h3,h4,h5,h6,h7]
 => ["H         H", "H         H", "H         H",
    "HHHHHHHHH", "H         H", "H         H", "H
    H"]
2.2.2 :025 > puts h
H         H
H         H
H         H
HHHHHHHHH
H         H
H         H
H         H
 => nil
```

You may be curious about that nil being returned at the end of the last puts command. It turns out that puts is just another method, and it doesn't return anything. Ruby represents that lack of value with the special nil value. You'll come across nil often as you learn more about programming with Ruby.

Creating the letter E

Next up is the letter E. You'll use the same general techniques that you just used for the letter H.

1. Create the first `e1` variable. Use nine E characters for the total size of the string:

```
2.2.2 :026 > e1 = "EEEEEEEEE"
 => "EEEEEEEEE"
```

2. Create the next variable, e2. This one is a little tricky, because for the vertical part of the letter E, you need to make sure that you account for both the visible part of the letter and the whitespace:

```
2.2.2 :027 > e2 = "E         "
 => "E         "
```

3. The letter E is pretty repetitive and uses one or the other of the two parts you've already created. Using the timesaving technique you learned for the previous letter, make the e3 variable the same as e2:

```
2.2.2 :028 > e3 = e2
 => "E         "
```

4. The fourth variable, e4, will store the middle horizontal part of the letter. For this project, make it the same as the top part:

```
2.2.2 :029 > e4 = e1
 => "EEEEEEEEE"
```

5. Time for some more whitespace, so make the next two variables store the same value as e2:

```
2.2.2 :030 > e5 = e2
 => "E         "
2.2.2 :031 > e6 = e2
 => "E         "
```

6. Now, create e7 to hold the bottom of the letter:

```
2.2.2 :032 > e7 = e1
 => "EEEEEEEEE"
```

7. Store the separate variables in an array and assign that to the variable e. Test it to make sure that it looks right:

```
2.2.2 :034 >    e = [e1,e2,e3,e4,e5,e6,e7]
 => ["EEEEEEEEE", "E          ", "E          ",
     "EEEEEEEEE", "E          ", "E          ",
     "EEEEEEEEE"]
2.2.2 :035 > puts e
EEEEEEEEE
E
E
EEEEEEEEE
E
E
EEEEEEEEE
 => nil
```

Creating the letter L

The letter L is even easier, because it's really only made of two unique parts. I'll show you a shortcut:

1. Create the first variable l1 (that's the lowercase letter L and the numeral for one):

```
2.2.2 :036 > l1 = "L          "
 => "L          "
```

2. Almost all of the letter L is made up of the same pattern as what we stored in l1, so you'll reuse that variable when you store it in an array. Instead, skip ahead to the seventh piece of the shape and create variable l7:

```
2.2.2 :037 > l7 = "LLLLLLLLL"
 => "LLLLLLLLL"
```

3. Now, create the 1 array by repeating the 11 variable six times. Once again, you end up saving a lot of typing!

```
2.2.2 :038 > l = [l1,l1,l1,l1,l1,l1,l7]
 => ["L          ", "L           ", "L            ", "L
      ", "L            ", "L             ", "LLLLLLLLL"]
```

4. Test the letter to make sure everything is formatted properly:

```
2.2.2 :039 > puts l
L
L
L
L
L
L
LLLLLLLLL
 => nil
```

Creating the letter O

The last letter array that you'll need to spell out HELLO is the letter O. The shape of the letter O is similar to a circle or oval, and you can take advantage of that symmetry when creating your letter parts.

1. Create variable o1 for the top of the letter:

```
2.2.2 :040 > o1 = "    OOO    "
 => "    OOO    "
```

2. Create o2:

```
2.2.2 :041 > o2 = "  O    O  "
 => "  O    O  "
```

3. Create o3:

```
2.2.2 :042 > o3 = " O      O "
 => " O      O "
```

4. Variables o4 and o5 are just repeating o3:

```
2.2.2 :043 > o4 = o3
 => "  O        O  "
2.2.2 :044 > o5 = o3
 => "  O        O  "
```

5. Variables o6 and o7 are the same as o2 and o1, respectively:

```
2.2.2 :045 > o6 = o2
 => "   O     O   "
2.2.2 :046 > o7 = o1
 => "     OOO     "
```

6. Create the letter O array and test:

```
2.2.2 :047 > o = [o1,o2,o3,o4,o5,o6,o7]
 => ["     OOO     ", "   O     O   ", "  O        O ", "  O
     O ", "  O        O ", "   O     O   ", "     OOO     "]
2.2.2 :048 > puts o
    OOO
   O     O
  O        O
  O        O
  O        O
   O     O
    OOO
 => nil
```

Combining the letters into a word

Now it's time to assemble HELLO. The first thing that comes to mind is to just use puts to print each array. puts can take a sequence of variables separated by commas.

Try printing your letters:

```
2.2.2 :049 > puts h, e, l, l, o
H         H
H         H
H         H
HHHHHHHHH
H         H
H         H
H         H
EEEEEEEEE
E
E
EEEEEEEEE
E
E
EEEEEEEEE
L
L
L
L
L
L
LLLLLLLLL
L
L
L
L
L
L
LLLLLLLLL
```

```
    OOO
  O     O
 O       O
 O       O
 O       O
  O     O
    OOO
=> nil
```

That sort of works, but it prints vertically. It would be nice if the letters were arranged horizontally to make it easy to read the word HELLO.

I'm going to show you something more advanced that takes advantage of the fact that our letters are all stored in arrays. Remember how I mentioned that arrays are like boxes with compartments? Well, it turns out you can get the contents of any of those contents by asking for the compartment number like this:

```
2.2.2 :050 > h[0]
 => "H        H"
2.2.2 :051 > h[1]
 => "H        H"
```

Here, you're providing the number of the compartment in square brackets next to the name of the array variable — h, in this case.

Notice that I started with the number zero in that first example: h[0]. Many programming languages, Ruby included, start counting at zero instead of one. As you becoming a more experienced programmer, you'll start to automatically count this way, too!

I've been calling the different storage areas of the array *compartments*. That isn't a technical term — it's just a way to think about it. Programmers call the different storage areas of an array *slots* or *cells,* among other terms. I usually use the term *slots* in the rest of this book.

Follow these steps to get the letters to print horizontally:

1. Combine the letters using string interpolation to access each array at the same time:

```
2.2.2 :053 > puts "#{h[0]} #{e[0]} #{l[0]} #{l[0]}
    #{o[0]}"
H         H EEEEEEEE L          L             OOO
  => nil
```

   You can sort of see how the letters are lining up. The problem is that if you use `puts` on separate lines in IRB, it won't look like the letter rows all connect. You need some way of repeating that command for each of the seven parts.

2. A more advanced technique that you'll use a lot in later projects is called *looping*. Looping is a way to have your code repeat itself a certain number of times. In Ruby, there is a handy looping method that you can call on numbers to count up to another number. Try this code:

```
2.2.2 :055 > 0.upto(6) do |count|
2.2.2 :056 >          puts h[count] + " " + e[count]
    + " " + l[count] + " " + l[count] + " " +
    o[count]
2.2.2 :057?>     end
```

   As soon as you press Return or Enter after the end line, you should see:

```
H         H EEEEEEEE L          L             OOO
H         H E        L          L           O     O
H         H E        L          L          O       O
HHHHHHHHH  EEEEEEEE L          L          O       O
H         H E        L          L          O       O
H         H E        L          L           O     O
H         H EEEEEEEE LLLLLLLLL  LLLLLLLLL    OOO
  => 0
```

Success! The first line, `0.upto(6) do |count|` starts the loop. It prepares Ruby to count starting at zero, up to and including six. As Ruby counts each number, it places the current number in the variable named `count`. Ruby then proceeds to the next line, which has your `puts` method. Inside of the string interpolation that combines all the letter parts, it asks for the zeroth one first, and prints that row. It then repeats six more times and prints each part in sequence (a total of seven). The final `end` line tells Ruby that the loop should stop there.

You'll learn more about the power of loops in the next couple of projects.

Trying Some Experiments

That was a lot of code! In this project, you got a rough idea of the power of working with strings. When you use strings in combination with basic arrays and even loops, you can create a powerful program.

To help you practice these new concepts, try some of these experiments:

- ✔ Create the letters that make up your name (or any word) and print them.

- ✔ Instead of using the string concatenation operator, +, try using string interpolation instead.

- ✔ Change the letters being used to lowercase letters without re-entering the values in each variable. *Hint:* Use the `downcase` method for a string.

Part II
Programmers Are Lazy! Stop Typing So Much!

```
● ● ●                    📁 project04 — bash — 80×24
About to draw a shape 10 big
using X for the edge
and o for the insider
          XX
         XooX
        XooooX
       XooooooX
      XooooooooX
     XooooooooooX
    XooooooooooooX
   XooooooooooooooX
  XooooooooooooooooX
XXXXXXXXXXXXXXXXXXXX
XXXXXXXXXXXXXXXXXXXX
XooooooooooooooooooX
XooooooooooooooooooX
XooooooooooooooooooX
XooooooooooooooooooX
XooooooooooooooooooX
XooooooooooooooooooX
XooooooooooooooooooX
XooooooooooooooooooX
XXXXXXXXXXXXXXXXXXXX
Christophers-MacBook-Pro:project04 chaupt$ ▌
```

In this part . . .

For debugging and troubleshooting tips for Ruby programs, go to www.dummies.com/extras/rubyforkids.

Shapes

In this project, you'll begin to use your programmer's editor to write code and get into the flow of programming, testing, and debugging your software using your terminal program.

You'll create a simple program that can generate a couple of geometric shapes using ASCII art to draw the outline and fill the shape with a pattern.

You'll also allow the user of your program to customize the output's size a bit by learning how to collect simple input from the user.

```
● ● ●                    project04 — bash — 80×24
About to draw a shape 10 big
using X for the edge
and . for the insider
        XX
      X..X
     X....X
    X......X
   X........X
  X..........X
 X............X
X..............X
X................X
XXXXXXXXXXXXXXXXXX
XXXXXXXXXXXXXXXXXX
X................X
X................X
X................X
X................X
X................X
X................X
X................X
X................X
XXXXXXXXXXXXXXXXXX
Christophers-MacBook-Pro:project04 chaupt$ ▊
```

Organizing a New Project

Up until this project, you've been using Interactive Ruby (IRB) to write and test your code. The nice thing about IRB is that you can get a feel for what the code is going to do immediately. This works great for small snippets of Ruby, but as you start to create more complicated programs, and as they get longer, IRB isn't very forgiving if you make typos or want to easily change or save your work.

In this project, you're going to start using Atom, the programmer's editor you installed in Project 1 to write and store code in files. You'll continue to use the terminal program to use a different Ruby command to run and test the code stored in the files you create.

Before each project, you'll want to get organized by keeping all your work for the project together in an easy-to-find place. You'll repeat these steps throughout this book, so now is a good time to get comfortable using the combination of your terminal program and your code editor.

If you haven't created a `development` folder already, refer to "Creating a development folder" in Project 2 for information on how to do that.

Follow these steps to create Project 4's folder:

1. Start your terminal program and enter the development folder:

   ```
   $ cd development
   ```

2. Create a new directory for this project:

   ```
   $ mkdir project04
   ```

3. Move in to the new directory:

   ```
   $ cd project04
   ```

4. Start Atom by double-clicking its icon.

   When Atom starts for the first time, it displays the Welcome tab and the Welcome Guide tab. You won't need these tabs during this project.

5. Click the Welcome Guide tab and choose File⇨Close Tab to close the Welcome Guide tab (see Figure 4-1). Repeat the process for the Welcome tab.

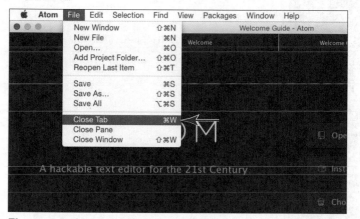

Figure 4-1: Close the Welcome Guide tab.

6. If you don't have one tab remaining called Untitled, choose File⇨New File to get a new file started (see Figure 4-2).

Figure 4-2: Use the New File menu option to create an empty Ruby file.

7. Even before you've written any code, save the file one time to make sure that it gets placed in the proper folder. To do that, choose File➪Save. A standard Save dialog box appears. Navigate to your `development` folder in your `home` directory and then choose the `project04` folder (see Figure 4-3). Name your file `shapes.rb` and click Save.

Figure 4-3: Use the Save dialog box to save your work.

8. Switch over to your terminal program and list out the files in the `project04` folder. On Mac, the command is:

```
$ ls
```

On Windows, the command is:

```
C:\Users\chris\development\project04> dir
```

Your prompt on Mac or Windows may look a little different than mine. That doesn't matter as long as you type the command correctly!

You should see `shapes.rb`. If not, make sure that you saved the file in the correct folder. Go back to Atom, choose File⇨ Save As, and navigate to the correct folder.

Now you're ready to write some code!

Printing versus Using puts

The first code you'll write will print out a message and then gather some input from your user.

When you were using IRB in earlier projects, you saw a couple of examples of using Ruby's built-in `puts` method, which prints a string for you. You'll use `puts` and another built-in output ori-ented method called `print` for the Shapes project. The `print` method is exactly like `puts`, but instead of automatically adding a newline character at the end of the string, `print` leaves the cursor on the same line at the end of the string.

A *newline character* (sometimes called a *carriage return, line feed,* or *line separator*) is an invisible character that instructs the termi-nal to move the current position at which it's displaying charac-ters down one line and all the way back to the left (by default). Newline, carriage return, and line feed are actually three different things, but I'll pretend they're the same for this book and use the term *newline*.

The cursor in the terminal is the current position at which the ter-minal is printing out characters or waiting for you to type. In your terminal program, the cursor's position is usually drawn as an underscore or block character. It may be blinking, too.

Follow these steps to start your program:

1. Switch to your Atom editor and make sure that you're looking at your new shapes.rb window. It should be blank.

2. Enter a comment at the top of the file as a reminder of what the program is going to do:

```
#
# Ruby For Kids Project 4: Shapes
# Programmed By: Chris Haupt
# Experiment with drawing ASCII art shapes using
    code.
#
```

Comments are labels, descriptions, explanations, or notes you put in your code to be read by you and other humans. Ruby doesn't try to interpret or run comments. You let Ruby know that a line is a comment by adding the hash character (#) before your comment starts. Sometimes it's useful to "comment out" code that isn't working or that you don't need but also don't want to delete from the file. You simply put a comment character in front of the lines you want to hide from Ruby.

3. Display a message to your user that will show up when the program is run:

```
puts "Welcome to Shapes"
print "How big do you want your shape? "
```

Getting Input with gets

The shapes program will need some information from the program's user. You could just write code that makes the shape the same size every time the program is run, but that wouldn't be very much fun.

Programmers call setting a variable to a single value that can't be changed *hard coding*. Hard-coded variables are sometimes necessary, but they aren't flexible. It's better when you can get input from your user to make the value *dynamic* (changeable on-the-fly) instead.

Ruby provides a number of ways to get input from the user. You'll use `gets` here. The `gets` method is basically the opposite of `puts` — instead of printing stuff, it gathers what the user types for you.

1. Right after the `print` statement in the last section, collect the user's input into a variable (`shape_size`):

```
print "How big do you want your shape? "
shape_size = gets
```

2. While you're here, gather some other input from the user that will be used to change the way the ASCII shape is drawn with different patterns:

```
print "Outside letter: "
outside_letter = gets
print "Inside letter: "
inside_letter = gets
```

3. Add some final lines to repeat back what the user entered before you start working on drawing the shape:

```
puts "About to draw a shape #{shape_size} big"
puts "using #{outside_letter} for the edge"
puts "and #{inside_letter} for the inside"
```

Now you're ready to try out the first part of your program.

Running the Program on the Command Line

Before you add more code, it's a really good idea to save and run your program. Programmers follow a pretty common practice of writing some code, running and testing the code, fixing bugs, and when everything is okay, writing some more new code.

By getting into this habit, you can check your own work and catch problems early on. It's much easier to find bugs in your code soon after you wrote the code that introduced the unexpected behavior.

1. Save your shapes.rb file by choosing File⇨Save.

2. Switch to your terminal program and make sure that you're still in the same directory as the shapes.rb file. Use the ls command (for Mac) or dir command (for Windows).

3. Run the program with Ruby by entering the following:

   ```
   $ ruby shapes.rb
   ```

   You should first see the welcome message you wrote, and then the cursor sitting waiting next to the first prompt (see Figure 4-4).

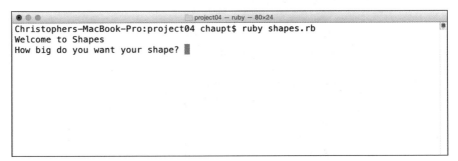

```
project04 — ruby — 80×24
Christophers-MacBook-Pro:project04 chaupt$ ruby shapes.rb
Welcome to Shapes
How big do you want your shape? ▌
```

Figure 4-4: The shapes programming waiting for your input.

If your program isn't running, or you see an error message of some kind, review your code in Atom and make sure you don't have any typos. Go back and review Project 2 and the section on figuring out what to do when things go wrong.

Chomping the newline away

Did you notice how the formatting of the output was a little strange? You probably expected the final message to be on three lines, but instead it was on six (as shown in the figure here). What happened?

```
● ● ●                    project04 — bash — 80×24
Christophers-MacBook-Pro:project04 chaupt$ ruby shapes.rb
Welcome to Shapes
How big do you want your shape? 10
Outside letter: X
Inside letter: o
About to draw a shape 10
 big
using X
  for the edge
and o
  for the insider
Christophers-MacBook-Pro:project04 chaupt$
```

You just discovered an interesting side effect of how `gets` works. When it listens for your input, it reads everything you type. *Everything!* That means that when you pressed Return or Enter at the end of your typing, an invisible newline character was also read and stored by `gets`. The variable holding your data values is also storing something you don't really want.

How do you get rid of it? The good news is that Ruby has all kinds of useful methods available to you. In fact, Ruby has one specifically for this newline problem called `chomp`. `chomp` is a useful method that comes with Ruby's string types, and it removes ending newline characters. Here's how it works:

1. Change the middle of your code with the prompts and `gets` code to look like this:

```
print "How big do you want your shape? "
shape_size = gets
```

(continued)

(continued)

```
shape_size = shape_size.chomp
print "Outside letter: "
outside_letter = gets
outside_letter = outside_letter.chomp
print "Inside letter: "
inside_letter = gets
inside_letter = inside_letter.chomp
```

2. Save changes by choosing File ➪ Save

3. Rerun your program and compare the results in the following figure to your own.

```
project04 — bash — 80×24
Christophers-MacBook-Pro:project04 chaupt$ ruby shapes.rb
Welcome to Shapes
How big do you want your shape? 10
Outside letter: X
Inside letter: o
About to draw a shape 10 big
using X for the edge
and o for the insider
Christophers-MacBook-Pro:project04 chaupt$ ▮
```

In the new code, Ruby reads your values into your variables and then immediately converts the variables' contents to remove the newline character.

Creating Code to Draw a Rectangle

Now it's time to create a rectangle on the screen using ASCII art. From the first part of the program, you've read in the user's preference for what size and letters to use to draw the shape, but how will the drawing part of the program work?

If you were going to draw a rectangle on paper that was filled in with a pattern, what would you need to do? First, you might draw the outline of the rectangle, and then you might color in the inside.

But for your program here, you'll want to instead draw the shape from the top to the bottom, one line at a time. How would you describe how to do that? Like this:

1. Draw the top of the rectangle using the outside (or edge) pattern for the first line.

2. For each of the lines that make up the sides and inside of the rectangle, draw the left edge, all of the middle, and then the right edge.

   Repeat this step until you need to draw the bottom of the rectangle.

3. Draw the bottom of the rectangle exactly as you drew the top edge.

What I just described is an algorithm for drawing rectangles line by line from top to bottom.

An *algorithm* is just a sequence of steps you follow to accomplish some task or calculation. In this case, you've written out the sequence to draw a rectangle by scanning across from top to bottom, line by line.

A first version of the rectangle

The Ruby version of your algorithm reads a lot like the English version I just wrote out:

1. Below the last line of the program, set up two variables that make it easier to see what's going on. You'll use the user's choice for shape size as both the height and width of the figure you're going to draw:

   ```
   height = shape_size
   width = shape_size
   ```

2. You'll be drawing the rectangle line by line, so set up a loop that will repeat your code for each row (so, that means you need your drawing code to run *height* times):

```
1.upto(height) do |row|
# Drawing code goes here
end
```

Loops are a powerful way to repeat code some number of times (or even an infinite number of times)! Ruby has several ways to program a loop. I'll show you more in future projects. The upto method is an easy way to count from a starting number to a final number. For the rectangle, you want to count starting at 1 for the first row and finishing counting when you reach the number represented by height.

3. Now, for the algorithm to work, you need to check to see what row you want the program to print. You have three cases: the first row, the middle rows, and the last row. Add in the case for the first row in the middle of your loop:

```
if row == 1
    puts outside_letter * width
end
```

If the row variable is equal to one, the program will use puts to print your choice for the outside_letter a number of times equal to width (you're reusing the technique you learned in Project 3 of multiplying a string by a number).

You use if statements when you want to see if some condition is true or false. The symbol == in Ruby asks the question: "Is the thing on the left side equal to the thing on the right side of the == symbol?" If it is, then Ruby will run the lines of code up until either another condition or an end keyword.

4. Next, add in a check to see if this is the last row. The elsif keyword starts another condition test, and you place it right

before the previous end keyword. That isn't a spelling mistake, by the way. Ruby just has a funny way of saying "else if"! The whole thing will look like this:

```
if row   == 1
    puts outside_letter * width
elsif row == height
    puts outside_letter * width
end
```

5. Finally, you need to handle the display of all the rows in the middle, so add one last condition using Ruby's else keyword. This code goes right before the end keyword. Here's the whole block of Ruby:

```
if row   == 1
  puts outside_letter * width
elsif row == height
  puts outside_letter * width
else
  middle = inside_letter * (width - 2)
  puts
    "#{outside_letter}#{middle}#{outside_letter}"
end
```

The middle case looks complicated. What's it doing? Well, according to your algorithm, it needs to draw the left and right edges and everything in the middle.

The middle variable is calculating the string that represents the center of the rectangle. If you take away one for the left edge character and one for the right edge character, the final width of the middle is the full width minus two characters.

The final puts statement uses the string processing you learned earlier to create the combined row.

6. Run your program and see if you have any errors. Do you get something like Figure 4-5? If you see an error that says something like `comparison of Fixnum with String failed`, this means Ruby had a hard time using the value inside `shape_size` as a number.

```
●●●                    project04 — bash — 80×24
Christophers-MacBook-Pro:project04 chaupt$ ruby shapes.rb
Welcome to Shapes
How big do you want your shape? 10
Outside letter: X
Inside letter: o
About to draw a shape 10 big
using X for the edge
and o for the insider
shapes.rb:24:in `>': comparison of Fixnum with String failed (ArgumentError)
        from shapes.rb:24:in `upto'
        from shapes.rb:24:in `<main>'
Christophers-MacBook-Pro:project04 chaupt$ ▊
```

Figure 4-5: Ruby isn't sure how to use strings for numbers.

Why is that a problem if you typed in a number? Well, `gets` reads in your input, but it reads all the characters you type as a string. You have to help Ruby convert the string to a number.

7. Change the two lines where you set the `height` and `width` variables to use the `to_i` method, which means convert this variable's contents into an integer (number):

```
height = shape_size.to_i
width = shape_size.to_i
```

Run your code again. Success (see Figure 4-6)!

A reusable rectangle

What if you wanted to draw two rectangles in a row? You could just copy the loop code and paste that code multiple times. Instead, you're going to put the rectangle code into your very first method.

```
● ● ●                     📄 project04 — bash — 80×24
Christophers-MacBook-Pro:project04 chaupt$ ruby shapes.rb
Welcome to Shapes
How big do you want your shape? 10
Outside letter: X
Inside letter: o
About to draw a shape 10 big
using X for the edge
and o for the insider
XXXXXXXXXX
XooooooooX
XooooooooX
XooooooooX
XooooooooX
XooooooooX
XooooooooX
XooooooooX
XooooooooX
XXXXXXXXXX
Christophers-MacBook-Pro:project04 chaupt$ ▌
```

Figure 4-6: Is this the world's most exciting rectangle?

Methods (also called *functions*) give you a way of storing and naming a piece of code and then using it later, possibly many times. You can pass different variables in to a method to change its behavior. You call variables passed to a method the method's *arguments* (no, not the shouting kind!).

Follow these steps to create a reusable method that will draw rectangles:

1. Start by adding a definition for our new rectangle method. Put this code at the top of your file right under the last comment:

    ```
    def rectangle(height, width, outside_letter,
        inside_letter)
      # The rectangle code will go here
    end
    ```

   The keyword `def` signals to Ruby that you're about to provide the definition of a method. `def` is followed by the name of the method (`rectangle`) and then a list of zero or more arguments — each argument being the name of a variable you can use inside of the method. You next provide the code that makes up the method's functionality and mark the end of the method with the keyword `end`.

2. Select the entire rectangle drawing loop code, choose Edit ⇨ Cut, and then choose Edit ⇨ Paste to paste that code inside of the method in place of the comment shown in Step 1:

```
def rectangle(height, width, outside_letter,
    inside_letter)
  1.upto(height) do |row|
    if row  == 1
      puts outside_letter * width
    elsif row == height
      puts outside_letter * width
    else
      middle = inside_letter * (width - 2)
      puts
    "#{outside_letter}#{middle}#{outside_letter}"
    end
  end
end
```

3. Now you can use the method you've created to draw a rectangle. To do this, you can *call* the method (in Ruby, this is also referred to as *sending* a message). At the bottom of your source code, after the lines that set the `width` and `height` variables, write this code:

```
rectangle(height, width, outside_letter,
    inside_letter)
```

Note that the variable names you use to call a method don't have to be named the same thing as what the arguments' names are. In this project, just to keep it simpler, they are the same. In later projects, the names won't always match. However, the position of the variables are important, and the first value you provide when calling a method goes into the first argument, the second into the second, and so on.

4. Run the program. It should look exactly like Figure 4-6 again.

5. Copy and paste the rectangle method call so you have two exact copies of that line, and run the program again. What happens?

Putting your code into methods allows you to easily reuse the code and makes it easier to change it or fix bugs. Imagine if you had pasted the long set of code for drawing a rectangle, twice, three times, or many, many times. (Try it!) This works, but if you have to make a small change to your code, you have to hunt down every version wherever it might be. With a method, you'd only have to fix it once!

Creating Code to Draw a Triangle

Now that you know about methods, you'll create a method that can draw a triangle. First, let's think about how this might work.

The triangle you'll draw will look like an isosceles triangle, where two sides will be the same size and the base will appear slightly smaller.

Unlike the rectangle, where each row was easy to format, for the triangle you need to make each row look different. The first row will be the top of the triangle (the pointy end). The last row will be the base of the triangle and will be the width that the user specifies.

I'll show you the code. See if you can figure out what it's doing.

1. Start a new method called `triangle` right after the `end` keyword of the `rectangle` method:

```
# Above here is the end of the rectangle method
def triangle( height, outside_letter,
    inside_letter)
# Code for the triangle will go here
end
```

Note that you'll be using the `height` variable for both the height and the width inside of this method.

2. Create a loop that will repeat `height` times. Put this code inside of the triangle method:

```
1.upto(height) do |row|
# Drawing code goes here in the next step
end
```

3. For a triangle, you need to draw *whitespace* (empty areas) for each row that doesn't take up the entire width that you're drawing. As you draw each row, you'll be drawing less whitespace. Add this line as the first line of your loop:

```
print ' ' * (height - row)
```

The math here will calculate a smaller number of spaces as the number of the row gets larger (remember, you're counting row 1 at the top, and row will equal the height at the bottom).

4. Next, you have to handle the case for the first row, which is the top of the triangle:

```
if row == 1
  puts "#{outside_letter * 2}"
end
```

Step 4's code goes immediately after Step 3.

5. Handle the last row case next by adding an `elsif` condition.

```
if row == 1
    puts "#{outside_letter * 2}"
  elsif row == height
    puts outside_letter * height * 2
  end
```

I'm showing you the entire condition here. You can just type in the `elsif` part if you like.

6. Now add the code for the slightly more complicated case of handling all the middle rows. For this last part of the condition, you'll use an `else` clause. See the entire condition here:

```ruby
if row == 1
  puts "#{outside_letter * 2}"
elsif row == height
  puts outside_letter * height * 2
else
  middle = inside_letter * (row - 2)
  print
    "#{outside_letter}#{middle}#{inside_letter}"
  puts
    "#{inside_letter}#{middle}#{outside_letter}"
end
```

The code looks a little strange. Why is there both a `print` and a `puts` statement?

7. It's time to display the triangle. At the very bottom of the code file, beneath the `rectangle` method call, add a `triangle` method call:

```ruby
triangle( height, outside_letter, inside_letter)
```

8. Save your program file, switch to your terminal, and run the program. You should see something like Figure 4-7.

```
● ● ●                    project04 — bash — 80×24
About to draw a shape 10 big
using X for the edge
and o for the insider
XXXXXXXXXX
XooooooooX
XooooooooX
XooooooooX
XooooooooX
XooooooooX
XooooooooX
XooooooooX
XooooooooX
XXXXXXXXXX
         XX
        XooX
       XooooX
      XoooooooX
     XooooooooooX
    XoooooooooooooX
   XooooooooooooooooX
  XoooooooooooooooooooX
XXXXXXXXXXXXXXXXXXXX
Christophers-MacBook-Pro:project04 chaupt$ ▊
```

Figure 4-7: A rectangle balanced on a triangle.

Drawing a House Using Your Two Shapes

You can play around with getting different final results by simply changing the order and number of times you call each method. In addition, by changing the values that you pass to the method's arguments, you can get even more combinations of shapes.

Let's try drawing a simple house:

1. Inside of your program, change your method calls so that the `triangle` method is called first, followed by the `rectangle` method:

```
triangle(height, outside_letter, inside_letter)
rectangle(height, width, outside_letter,
    inside_letter)
```

2. Save and run your program, and you should get something similar to Figure 4-8.

```
● ● ●                    📁 project04 — bash — 80×24
About to draw a shape 10 big
using X for the edge
and o for the insider
        XX
       XooX
      XooooX
     XoooooooX
    XooooooooX
   XoooooooooX
  XooooooooooooX
 XoooooooooooooX
 XooooooooooooooX
XXXXXXXXXXXXXXXXXXXX
XXXXXXXXX
XooooooooX
XooooooooX
XooooooooX
XooooooooX
XooooooooX
XooooooooX
XooooooooX
XooooooooX
XXXXXXXXX
Christophers-MacBook-Pro:project04 chaupt$ ▉
```

Figure 4-8: Not quite a house.

3. The main part of the house isn't as wide as the base of your triangle, so it looks like the roof might fall off! How would you fix that? It seems like the rectangle should use twice the width that it is currently using, so you should change that. Multiple the width for the rectangle by 2:

```
triangle(height, outside_letter, inside_letter)
rectangle(height, width * 2, outside_letter,
    inside_letter)
```

Whoa! Yes you can do simple math inside of a method call's argument list. Ruby will calculate the value for twice the width before it calls the method for you.

4. Save and run your program. Now how does the house look? It should look like Figure 4-9.

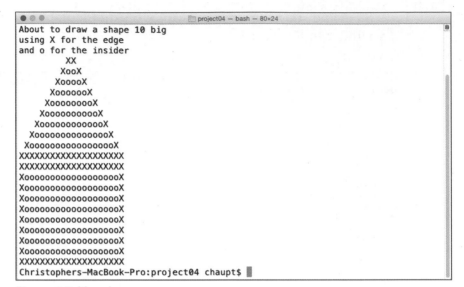

```
● ● ●                         project04 — bash — 80×24
About to draw a shape 10 big
using X for the edge
and o for the insider
        XX
       XooX
      XooooX
     XooooooX
    XooooooooX
   XoooooooooooX
  XooooooooooooX
 XoooooooooooooX
XooooooooooooooooX
XXXXXXXXXXXXXXXXXX
XXXXXXXXXXXXXXXXXX
XooooooooooooooooX
XooooooooooooooooX
XooooooooooooooooX
XooooooooooooooooX
XooooooooooooooooX
XooooooooooooooooX
XooooooooooooooooX
XooooooooooooooooX
XXXXXXXXXXXXXXXXXX
Christophers-MacBook-Pro:project04 chaupt$
```

Figure 4-9: Your house.

Testing Your Program

When you get more comfortable with programming, you get into a regular rhythm of working. First, you think about the problem you want to solve. Then you write some code that you think will work. Finally, you save and run your program to see if you were right.

This cycle of thinking, coding, and testing is repeated over and over again. This is exactly how professional programmers work. If during your testing you find a bug or want to make a change, you simply start the cycle again: Think about how to fix it, code the fix, and test again!

In future projects, I'll encourage you to save frequently and try running your program, even if it isn't quite done yet. You may catch errors when you do this. But catching problems early on when you first write new code is the easiest time to fix them.

Trying Some Experiments

You've learned a lot of new things in this project. You used some of the string tricks from earlier projects, and added more conditions, loops, and now methods to your toolbox. These basic building blocks are enough to write any program you can imagine. Later projects in this book show you more ways to use these beginning concepts, sometimes with shortcuts, and sometimes as ways to make writing and maintaining your code easier.

With your shape program, try a few experiments.

✔ How would you draw three triangles, one on top another using a loop?

✔ What if you wanted to draw an upside-down triangle? Create a method called `flipped_triangle`, and have it draw with the pointed end on the bottom.

✔ You may have noticed that the triangle code actually draws *two* triangles back to back. Experiment with the code to see if you can separate out and draw only one of them (a right triangle for you geometry students out there).

✔ Can you come up with a new shape method?

Simple Adventure

For this project, you build a turn-based text adventure game that changes every time you play it. Your player will be trapped inside a randomly generated cavern, be able to find treasure, and occasionally have to defeat a monster.

This project is more involved than your prior projects, but it takes advantage of everything you've learned up until now. You'll get more experience breaking up code into methods that can be reused throughout your program. You'll also see that methods can be used to hide complicated lines of Ruby to make reading your overall code easier.

```
project05 — bash — 80×24
Room number 5
You are in a small green tomb. There is an exit on the east wall.
What do you do? (m - move, s - search): s
You look, but don't find anything.

Room number 5
You are in a small green tomb. There is an exit on the east wall.
Oh no! An evil monster is in here with you!
What do you do? (m - move, s - search, f - fight): s
You found an enchanted sword!

Room number 5
You are in a small green tomb. There is an exit on the east wall.
Oh no! An evil monster is in here with you!
What do you do? (m - move, s - search, f - fight): m

Room number 6
You are in a tiny blue cave. There is an exit on the east wall.
What do you do? (m - move, s - search): m

You escaped!
You explored 7 rooms
and found 2 treasures.
Christophers-MacBook-Pro:project05 chaupt$
```

Organizing a New Project

In this project, you continue to use Atom to create and edit your source code file. You use the terminal program to run and play the Adventure game.

Project 5 will be stored in one Ruby file.

If you haven't created a development folder already, refer to Project 2 for information on how to do that.

1. Start your terminal program and enter the development folder:

   ```
   $ cd development
   ```

2. Create a new directory for this project:

   ```
   $ mkdir project05
   ```

3. Move into the new directory:

   ```
   $ cd project05
   ```

4. Start Atom by double-clicking its icon.

5. Create a new source code file by choosing File ⇨ New File.

6. Save it by choosing File ⇨ Save, and store it in your project05 directory. Call the file adventure.rb.

If some of these steps are confusing to you, refer to the "Organizing a New Project" section in Project 4. It provides more details for each step.

Now you're ready to create your adventure game.

Planning the Project

Before you write one line of code, let's think about the steps that this program needs to take to create an adventure game. It's a turn-based, text adventure game, so everything will happen in the terminal window. But what exactly will it do?

First, the program needs to set up variables that keep track of the player. For this game, you'll track the player's health, how much treasure she found, what room she is in, and whether she escaped yet from the cavern.

The program should welcome the player, tell her what's going on, and perhaps tell her how to play.

Each turn, the program should

- Check to see whether the player is still alive and hasn't escaped.

- Check to see if a monster has shown up, and if so, let the monster and the player battle it out if desired.

- Allow the player to look for treasure.

- Let the player leave the room and go to another room.

The program should

- Make sure that different rooms have unique descriptions.

- Know how to randomly decide if monsters show up.

- Determine randomly whether the player found treasure.

When the player takes too much damage or escapes the cavern, the program should display an appropriate final message.

Wow, that's a lot! In this project, you'll break this down into small bits of Ruby and see that it isn't actually too hard to create such a feature-rich game.

Now it's time to jump in and create some code!

Looking at the Program Skeleton

The first thing you're going to do is to create some of the main parts of the program that manage the game. Later, you'll fill this all in with the code that creates the cool features you planned out earlier.

1. In Atom, add a short comment at the top of your `adventure.rb` Ruby file to describe what the project is about.

   I used this, but you can write whatever you like:

   ```
   #
   # Ruby For Kids Project 5: Simple Adventure
   # Programmed By: Chris Haupt
   # A random text adventure game.
   #
   ```

2. Next, set up some starting values for variables you'll use to run the game.

   I'll explain what each of these variables is as we use them, but they should be mostly self-explanatory:

   ```
   number_of_rooms_explored  = 1
   treasure_count            = 0
   damage_points             = 5
   escaped                   = false
   monster                   = false
   current_room              = ""
   ```

3. Write the code that will introduce the player to the game, and put it below the comments:

```
puts "You are trapped in the dungeon. Collect
    treasure and try to escape"
puts "before an evil monster gets you!"
puts "To play, type one of the command choices on
    each turn."
puts ""
```

When this book is printed, some lines will be wrapped around to look like two lines. You should make the strings you see here and elsewhere all on one line in your code editor.

4. You'll be using a special loop to run the main part of the game, so for now, add a placeholder for that code — you'll fill in the details later:

```
while damage_points > 0 and not escaped do
    # Game code will go here
end
```

The loop itself is a `while` loop. The `while` loop takes a condition that's very similar to the condition used in an `if` statement. The loop will continue while the condition is true. In this code, you're testing whether the player's `damage_points` variable is still greater than zero (he's alive) and if he hasn't escaped from the dungeon (the `escaped` variable is set to `false`).

5. Write some code that will display the final results of the game when the player has either escaped or met an untimely end. Put this code immediately after the `end` keyword from the `while` loop:

```
if damage_points > 0
  puts "You escaped!"
```

```
    puts "You explored #{number_of_rooms_explored}
      rooms"
    puts "and found #{treasure_count} treasures."
  else
    puts "OH NO! You didn't make it out!"
    puts "You explored #{number_of_rooms_explored}
      rooms"
    puts "before meeting your doom."
  end
```

The condition at the end of the code is used to select one of two final messages for the player. If the player is still healthy (the `damage_points` variable is greater than zero), the player must have escaped, so you print out a successful message. If the player's damage is less than or equal to zero, he hasn't done so well.

6. Now is a good time to test your code to see what happens. You might even find a typo or two. Save the program and switch over to your terminal and run the project:

```
$ ruby adventure.rb
```

What happens? Do you get any errors? If so, check your typing and use the debugging hints found earlier in the book. Does your program just freeze after printing out the initial message (even if you type something)? That's what mine does. Why is that? Press Ctrl+C to force the project to stop (see Figure 5-1).

What you just found is called an *infinite loop,* which is any kind of code that continuously repeats itself without ever ending. In the case of your current code, the `while` loop is constantly checking to see if either of the two parts of the condition are false. Because you haven't written the code to change these variables, Ruby will just keep trying forever.

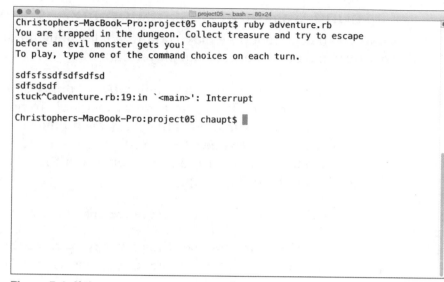

```
Christophers-MacBook-Pro:project05 chaupt$ ruby adventure.rb
You are trapped in the dungeon. Collect treasure and try to escape
before an evil monster gets you!
To play, type one of the command choices on each turn.

sdfsfssdfsdfsdfsd
sdfsdsdf
stuck^Cadventure.rb:19:in `<main>': Interrupt

Christophers-MacBook-Pro:project05 chaupt$
```

Figure 5-1: If the program appears stuck, press Ctrl+C to stop it.

Creating the Main Game Loop

For the adventure project, you're going to start creating the main game loop first, where the rules and input and output of the game are. Then you'll create small methods to implement the functionality you need to run the game. You'll program as if these methods already exist and use Ruby to help fill in the missing functionality.

There are a number of ways to write code when implementing a complicated project. Two common ones are *top-down* and *bottom-up* programming. In this project, you're starting at the top, building the bigger concepts first, and assuming you'll fill in the lower-level methods that you need. You could also write the lower-level simple methods first, and then use them as you build them up into the bigger pieces. That would be bottom-up development.

Creating the room description and actions

First, you'll need to let the player know what's going on during that turn and describe what the player can do.

1. Each turn, the player will have a number of options of what to do on her turn. You'll use the `actions` variable to hold these choices in an array and reset the array each time you run through the game engine's loop. You'll use the `actions` array to build a little menu for the user shortly. Put the following code inside the `while` loop:

   ```
   actions = ["m - move", "s - search"]
   ```

2. Print out what room number the player is currently in using the count you're storing in `number_of_rooms_explored`:

   ```
   puts "Room number #{number_of_rooms_explored}"
   ```

3. You'll use a method you write later to generate a new room in the cavern. For now, just print out the empty variable you set up earlier:

   ```
   puts current_room
   ```

4. Now check to see whether there is a monster in the room and, if so, print out a message and add another action for the player (the ability to fight the monster!):

   ```
   if monster
     puts "Oh no! An evil monster is in here with
       you!"
     actions << "f - fight"
   end
   ```

5. Finally, display the actions menu for the player so she knows what she can do:

   ```
   print "What do you do? (#{actions.join(', ')}): "
   ```

The menu will be the last thing the player sees before you ask her for her game command. The `print` statement will leave the cursor on the same line and show a handy little menu to remind the player of her choices.

You're using a nice little method that is provided to you by Ruby's array object called `join`. The `join` method will take all the items inside of the array and connect them together into one string, using the parameter you provide as the connecting string. In this case, all the strings inside the array are joined together with commas.

Be careful with all those symbols in that string. This is an easy place to make a typo.

6. Save your code and test. You'll still have an infinite loop, but this time you can see your output fly by over and over again (see Figure 5-2). Use Ctrl+C to stop the program.

```
● ● ●                    📄 project05 — bash — 80×24
What do you do? (m — move, s — search): Room number 1

What do you do? (m — move, s — search): Room number 1

What do you do? (m — move, s — search): Room number 1

What do you do? (m — move, s — search): Room number 1

What do you do? (m — move, s — search): Room number 1

What do you do? (m — move, s — search): Room number 1

What do you do? (m — move, s — search): Room number 1

What do you do? (m — move, s — search): Room number 1

What do you do? (m — move, s — search): Room number 1

adventure.rb:27:in `write': Interrupt
        from adventure.rb:27:in `print'
        from adventure.rb:27:in `<main>'

Christophers-MacBook-Pro:project05 chaupt$ ▊
```

Figure 5-2: An infinite number of messages.

Responding to player actions

Now it's time to get the player's command choice and have the game respond to it.

1. Collect the player's command choice by using the `gets` method, and then see if a monster is present and if it takes action against the player. Continue to place the following code inside of the `while` loop after the previous section's code:

```
player_action = gets.chomp
if monster and monster_attack?
  damage_points = damage_points - 1
  puts "OUCH, the monster bit you!"
end
```

You're using the `chomp` method here because you don't want the trailing new line character that the `gets` method returns.

2. The player will enter her commands by typing a single letter that is shorthand for the action. If the player wants to move out of the current room of the cavern, she'll use the letter M. Create a condition to check that and add the code you'll use for the move command:

```
if player_action == "m"
  current_room = create_room
  number_of_rooms_explored =
    number_of_rooms_explored + 1
  monster = has_monster?
  escaped = has_escaped?
```

That's a lot of stuff. What's going on? When the player moves, a number of things happen at the same time. First, you need to generate a new room to explore. You'll use a method that you create later called `create_room` and save the results into the `current_room` variable. Next, you'll add one to the `number_of_rooms_explored` variable. Then you'll check to see if the new room has a monster in it by using your `has_monster?` method. Finally, you'll also check to see if by chance the player has found the exit and escaped using the method `has_escaped?`.

Ruby allows you to use the ? and the ! punctuation marks in method names. Often, the question mark is used in a name to signal to the programmer that the method will return a *Boolean* value, which is either `true` or `false`.

3. If the player chooses to search the room, she'll use the letter S. Create the condition and code that handles searching:

```
elsif player_action == "s"
  if has_treasure?
    puts "You found #{treasure}!"
    treasure_count = treasure_count + 1
  else
    puts "You look, but don't find anything."
  end
  # when you look for treasure,
  # you might attract another monster!
  if not monster
    monster = has_monster?
  end
```

You're using a few new methods that you'll create in this case. First, you check to see if the room `has_treasure?` and depending on the answer, you'll print out the correct message. Regardless of whether the player found treasure, spending more time in the room searching around may attract the attention of a new monster, so you check to see if the room already has a monster!

You've probably noticed some conditions have the keyword `not` in them. When used in front of a Boolean value, it reverses its meaning. That is, `not true` means `false` and vice versa. Most of the conditions you write in this book can be read out loud and will usually make sense.

4. The last command you'll support is the fight command represented by the letter F. Add a condition to support it now:

```ruby
elsif player_action == "f"
  if defeat_monster?
    monster = false
    puts "You defeated the scary monster!"
  else
    puts "You attack and MISS!!!"
  end
```

Here you use a new method called `defeat_monster?` that will check to see whether the player wins in a fight against the monster. In either case, you print out a message to let the player know what happened.

5. Handle the case if the player enters a command that you don't support:

```ruby
else
  puts "I don't know how to do that!"
end
puts ""
```

The final `puts` at the end just makes everything look a little better.

6. Save and run again. This time, you get a menu and can actually do something! Of course, as soon as you enter a command, what happens? Ruby let's you know that you have some work to do (see Figure 5-3). Note that the error you see may be different depending on what choice you make in the menu. That's okay!

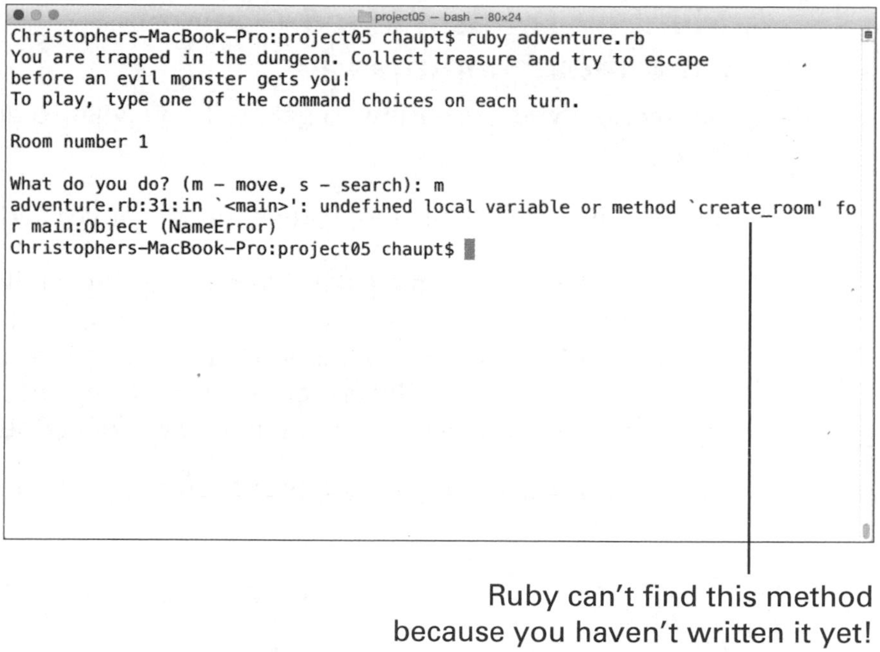

```
● ● ●                    project05 — bash — 80×24
Christophers-MacBook-Pro:project05 chaupt$ ruby adventure.rb
You are trapped in the dungeon. Collect treasure and try to escape
before an evil monster gets you!
To play, type one of the command choices on each turn.

Room number 1

What do you do? (m - move, s - search): m
adventure.rb:31:in `<main>': undefined local variable or method `create_room' fo
r main:Object (NameError)
Christophers-MacBook-Pro:project05 chaupt$ █
```

Ruby can't find this method
because you haven't written it yet!

Figure 5-3: The player can now see a menu of choices, but Ruby shows an error.

Creating Game Rules Methods

When Ruby displayed an error at the end of the last section, it
was telling you that a method was missing. You'll now start to fix
this problem by coding up the methods that contain the "rules" of
your game.

The main game loop is already a big piece of code. As you gain
experience, you'll figure out ways to shrink it down by moving
some of the code into other methods.

By keeping methods small, it's easier to test them, and it's easier
to understand what's going on just by looking at them. Ruby lets
you name methods pretty much anything. By choosing names that
mean something in the context of the program you're writing, the
code can actually read very closely to the English meaning of the
words.

Adding methods needed
for the move command

In this section, you'll use Ruby to help tell you what to do in
each step.

1. Run the program again and choose the M (move) action.

   You should see something like Figure 5-3. Ruby is telling you it
   can't find the `create_room` variable or method. At this point,
   Ruby can't tell what your intention was for `create_room`, so
   it mentions two possibilities. You want `create_room` to be a
   method that will create a random new room description.

   Add this method definition right after the topmost comments:

   ```
   def create_room
     "You are in a room. There is an exit on the
       wall."
   end
   ```

   This method will return the string when called. Yes, that's kind
   of boring. You'll make it more interesting in the next section.

   In other languages, you usually have to explicitly say what
   value you want to return from a method or function. In Ruby,
   you can spell that out with the keyword `return`, but Ruby will
   also automatically send back the value of the last statement in
   a method. Because the room description string is the last line
   in the method, that's what Ruby sends back.

2. Use the `create_room` method to initialize the first room the
   player will visit. Change the definition of the `current_room`
   variable to use the value of the method instead of an empty
   string:

   ```
   current_room              = create_room
   ```

3. Save and test to find the next method that needs to be programmed.

   Looks like it's a check for `has_monster?`.

4. Add `has_monster?` right below the `create_room` method near the top:

   ```
   def has_monster?
     if roll_dice(2, 6) >= 8
       true
     else
       false
     end
   end
   ```

   This method uses yet another method you need to create to implement its rule. The `roll_dice` method will take two arguments: one for the number of dice to roll and the other for the kind of dice (number of sides). For this adventure game, all the rules are based on rolling pretend dice. `has_monster?` will find a monster if the virtual roll of two six-sided dice is eight or more.

5. Might as well create the `roll_dice` method now, because you'll need it a lot.

   ```
   def roll_dice(number_of_dice, size_of_dice)
     total = 0
     1.upto(number_of_dice) do
       total = total + rand(size_of_dice) + 1
     end
     return total
   end
   ```

   The method looks a little complicated, but if you break it down, it isn't too bad. You're using a loop to repeat the "rolling of the die" for the number of times requested. The `upto` method is the same as you used in earlier projects. The new method called `rand` will give you a random number between zero and the size of the dice. Since you don't want zero, you have to add one. You total up all the rolls to get the final number.

I'm showing you the `return` statement here as an example. You don't need to use the explicit `return`, but you can if you want to.

Random numbers in programming are really useful things. In your game, random numbers are simulating rolling dice. Later in this project, you'll see other ways to get random values. Randomness makes your game act differently each time you play because you can't predict exactly what's going to happen. That is way more fun!

6. You need one more method, `has_escaped?` for the movement command:

```ruby
def has_escaped?
  if roll_dice(2, 6) >= 11
    true
  else
    false
  end
end
```

7. Run the game.

You should now be able to press the M command multiple times, and maybe even go through multiple rooms. Eventually you'll run into a Ruby undefined method error like Figure 5-4. It is time to handle monster combat!

Yes! You were able to move...

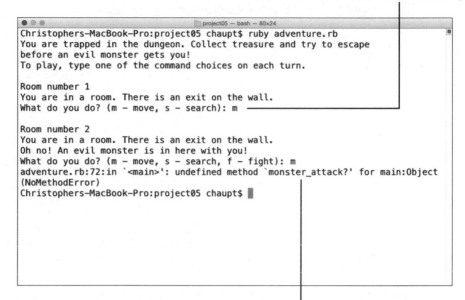

...but Ruby tells you it can't find another method.

Figure 5-4: You can mostly move now, but the monster causes an error!

Adding methods for handling the fighting monster

Now is the time for handling both the monster attacking the player and the player being able to fight back. You'll again use the roll_dice method to help determine the outcome of the action.

1. Add in the monster_attack? method to see if the monster will attack the player:

```
def monster_attack?
  if roll_dice(2, 6) >= 9
    true
  else
    false
  end
end
```

By setting the needed dice roll on two six-sided dice to nine or higher, it's hard for the monster to attack.

2. Next, add in a method to see if the player successfully defeats the monster:

```
def defeat_monster?
  if roll_dice(2, 6) >= 4
    true
  else
    false
  end
end
```

You're making it easy for the player to defeat the monster here, using the value four as the needed dice roll.

3. Run the program again. You should now be able to move (M) and fight (F) if a monster is present. Everything seems to be working until you decide to look for treasure. Let's add that next.

Adding methods for treasure searches

The last major piece of functionality for the adventure game is to allow the player to look for treasure. The main game loop needs one more method.

1. Add the has_treasure? method now:

```
def has_treasure?
  if roll_dice(2, 6) >= 8
    true
  else
    false
  end
end
```

2. The treasure case in the game loop also needs a method to generate an interesting name for the treasure. Add a method simply called `treasure`:

```
def treasure
  ["gold coins", "gems", "a magic wand", "an
    enchanted sword"].sample
end
```

Here, you're using another tool that Ruby gives you to make a random choice. The `sample` method is associated with an *array*. It will randomly pick one of the choices inside the array. Because your array is full of strings that describe treasure, you can get different results each time the `treasure` method is called in the game. This makes the search for treasure much more interesting!

3. Run the game one more time. It should be completely working now (see Figure 5-5).

```
●●●                    project05 — ruby — 80×24
You are trapped in the dungeon. Collect treasure and try to escape
before an evil monster gets you!
To play, type one of the command choices on each turn.

Room number 1
You are in a room. There is an exit on the wall.
What do you do? (m — move, s — search): m

Room number 2
You are in a room. There is an exit on the wall.
Oh no! An evil monster is in here with you!
What do you do? (m — move, s — search, f — fight): s
OUCH, the monster bit you!
You found an enchanted sword!

Room number 2
You are in a room. There is an exit on the wall.
Oh no! An evil monster is in here with you!
What do you do? (m — move, s — search, f — fight): f
You defeated the scary monster!

Room number 2
You are in a room. There is an exit on the wall.
What do you do? (m — move, s — search): ▊
```

Figure 5-5: A complete game (almost!).

Creating Game Helper Methods

The game is technically complete, and you can test it and look for any bugs by trying all the different player actions in various combinations.

One common task after the basic game is done is to add a little polish to make it more interesting. You already did a little of this by making a `treasure` method that randomly picked a goodie for the player. Now you'll make a set of methods that will generate rooms that are less boring.

1. Replace the `create_room` method with this one:

```
def create_room
  "You are in a #{size} #{color} #{room_type}.
    There is an exit on the #{direction} wall."
end
```

This version uses some other helper methods to create some variety. You'll create the code for these next.

Helper methods are usually small pieces of code that help the programmer get some often repetitive task done. Sometimes these methods are called *utility methods* and are used to tidy up a program.

2. Add a `size` helper method to create a randomly selected room size description:

```
def size
  ["huge", "large", "big", "regular", "small",
    "tiny"].sample
end
```

3. Create another helper for picking a color:

```
def color
  ["red", "blue", "green", "dark", "golden",
    "crystal"].sample
end
```

4. Write a method to select a room type:

```
def room_type
   ["cave",  "treasure room",  "rock cavern",
      "tomb", "guard room", "lair"].sample
end
```

5. And finally, for fun, code up a method to pick a direction:

```
def direction
   ["north", "south", "east", "west"].sample
end
```

6. Save and run your program.

How does that look (see Figure 5-6)? It is funny how a little description makes the game feel much more interesting and different each time you play.

Much more interesting!

```
● ● ●                       📄 project05 — bash — 80×24
What do you do? (m - move, s - search): m

Room number 2
You are in a large crystal tomb. There is an exit on the east wall. ───
Oh no! An evil monster is in here with you!
What do you do? (m - move, s - search, f - fight): m

Room number 3
You are in a huge blue lair. There is an exit on the west wall. ───
What do you do? (m - move, s - search): s
You look, but don't find anything.

Room number 3
You are in a huge blue lair. There is an exit on the west wall.
What do you do? (m - move, s - search): m

Room number 4
You are in a tiny dark rock cavern. There is an exit on the south wall. ──
What do you do? (m - move, s - search): m

You escaped!
You explored 5 rooms
and found 0 treasures.
Christophers-MacBook-Pro:project05 chaupt$ ▊
```

Figure 5-6: A much more interesting set of rooms.

Trying Some Experiments

You did it! You created a full (little) adventure game using Ruby! With the techniques you've used in this project, you can create all kinds of games.

The adventure game in this project is just the start. There are many experiments you can try:

- The player might get tired of playing, so add a `quit` command (Q) to the menu and make the main game loop stop running when it's used.

- Play with the different settings for the game rules. Does the game get more or less fun if you change how often the monster attacks or how easy it is to find treasure?

- Add more descriptions for the room generator.

- Create a "monster generator" that makes the description of the monster more interesting.

- Come up with a different action the player could take and add that feature to the game.

Number Guessing

Guessing numbers is pretty simple, but what happens when the person giving you clues isn't telling the truth? In this project, you'll write code in which the computer picks a number and the player tries to guess the number in the fewest moves.

This project introduces a new way to start to organize your code. You'll learn more about objects and classes, which give you a way to store data and methods together in a way that helps you think more clearly about the problem you're trying to solve. In the number guessing game, you'll start by simply splitting the program into the player part and the game part.

```
● ● ●                        project06 — ruby — 79×24

What is your name? Chris

------> Round #1

I'll pick a number between 1 and what number? 10
How many guesses do you think it will take?
(average would be 3): 4

Chris, what is your guess? 5
HINT: You are too low
Guess count: 1 target: 4

Chris, what is your guess? 7
HINT: You are too high
Guess count: 2 target: 4

Chris, what is your guess? 6
YEAH!!!!! You guessed it!
Guess count: 3 target: 4

------> Round #2

I'll pick a number between 1 and what number? █
```

Organizing a New Project

You'll use Atom to create and edit your source code, and you'll store this project in a single Ruby file. You'll use the terminal program to run and play the number guessing game.

If you haven't created a development folder already, refer to Project 2 for instructions.

Follow these steps to set up your source code directory and file for this project:

1. Start your terminal program and enter the development folder:

   ```
   $ cd development
   ```

2. Create a new directory for this project:

   ```
   $ mkdir project06
   ```

3. Move in to the new directory:

   ```
   $ cd project06
   ```

4. Start Atom by double-clicking its icon.

5. Create a new source code file by choosing File⇨New File.

6. Save the file by choosing File⇨Save, and store it in your project06 directory. Call the file guess.rb.

If some of these steps are confusing to you, refer to the "Organizing a New Project" section in Project 4. It provides more detail for each step.

Now you're ready to create your number guessing game.

Planning the Project

This project sounds simple enough: guessing a number that the computer is "thinking of." What makes it challenging? There are a couple of new techniques that I'll show you as you code this project. You'll divide the work into two main objects: one representing the player and the other representing the computer game engine. For this game, the computer does most of the work, and the player really just provides some information (like number guesses) to the engine. Unlike prior projects, you'll notice that more and more of the data and coding is hidden away in these objects.

So, what does the overall program need to do? The program will be made up of several parts: the overall program, the player code, and the game engine code. The overall program sets things up and uses the other two parts to manage the player and the game's progress and rules. The player object will keep track of its name, guesses, and score. The game object will manage all the rules and tell the player to do various things at the right time.

The program should welcome the player, tell him what's going on, and perhaps tell him how to play. The overall program will set up the player and game objects and connect them so they can interact.

Each turn, the game object should check to see if the current round or the overall game is complete.

At the start of a new round, the game object should ask the player for the biggest number it should use for the range of numbers it will use to select its secret number. Also at the start of a new round, the game object should ask the player how many guesses the player thinks he'll need to guess the secret number. The game will use this guess later to calculate a score (fewer guesses is better).

The game will proceed to run a round of the game. During a round, the game will ask the player for a new guess. The game will see if the player's guess is higher, lower, or the correct number. The game will give the player some score if he guessed the number.

If the player didn't guess the correct number, the game will prepare a hint as to whether the player is too high or too low. There will be a chance that the game will lie to the user about this hint!

The game will run multiple rounds of the game. When the last round is done, the game will display the final score for the player.

For such a simple game, there are a lot of steps when you break it down in terms of logic and how a program will behave. Ruby will make this coding as simple as possible, but you'll get a chance to see a new way to organize your work. These new techniques will make the more advanced projects later in the book easier to understand and program.

Looking at the Program Skeleton

Like with your previous projects, you'll start by sketching out a basic program and fill in the details as you go. Because I'll be teaching you some very basic object-oriented programming techniques, the code will start to be arranged in a new way that moves most of the data (variables) and methods into something called a *class*. A class acts like a template that describes an object and allows you to set one up and start using it.

Object-oriented programming (OOP) is one of a number of ways that computer programmers use to organize complicated software into pieces of functionality that make it easier to think, plan, build, debug, and maintain the software. When thinking in an object-oriented way, you'll try to identify the objects, which are like nouns in a sentence (for example, dog, cat, car, computer), and the objects' behaviors, which are like the verbs in a sentence (for example, play, drive, eat, sleep). Ruby is an object-oriented programming language, and you'll see over time that everything in Ruby is an object, and you get these objects to *do something* by sending them a *message* (which is to say, calling a *method*).

Start the program's main code:

1. Go in to Atom in your `guess.rb` file and add a basic comment to describe what the program is all about:

```
#
# Ruby For Kids Project 6: Guessing Game
# Programmed By: Chris Haupt
# A guessing game in which the hints might not be
    true
#
```

2. Create a helpful message that explains to the player what's about to happen:

```
puts "Welcome to the Guessing Game"
puts "We will play #{Game::TOTAL_ROUNDS} rounds.
    Try to guess the number"
puts "I'm thinking of in the fewest guesses."
puts "You'll also estimate how many guesses it
    will take."
puts "If you do it in fewer guesses, you'll gain
    bonus points!"
puts ""
```

One unusual bit of code in the welcome message is the variable TOTAL_ROUNDS that you include in the second line. Ruby programmers use the convention that a variable spelled in all capital letters means it is a *constant*. A constant is a variable that will be set once and never changed. In this project, the constant holds the number of rounds you want the game to run (three for now). By using a constant, if you ever want to change the behavior of the game, you simply change the constant value once, and everywhere it's used, it's automatically up to date. This is easier than hunting down all the places in the game you might use the number 3 and figuring out if you should change it.

3. Unlike prior projects, there will only be a few variables in the main code, and they'll mostly be used to hold the two objects you're going to create:

```
print "What is your name? "
name   = gets.chomp
player = Player.new(name)
game   = Game.new(player)
```

What's going on here? The first two lines should be familiar to you. You prompt the user for his name, and then chomp off the new line character.

The next two lines are a little different. Here you're creating your two required objects from their classes, which I call Player and Game. By calling the new method on those classes, and passing some variables, you're telling Ruby to create and set up one object of each type. Don't worry about the details for now — just know that when you see that new method, you're telling Ruby that you want a new object of that kind.

4. Now you can write the main game loop, which I'll show you in a few parts. This time around, most of the work is going to be done inside the objects you create, and the main code is just going to use that functionality to create the loop itself:

```
while !game.done? do
  puts ""
  puts "------> Round ##{game.round}"
  puts ""
```

You're starting the loop and then printing a message that will show at the start of each round.

You're using a familiar `while` loop here, but with a slightly different syntax than last time. You can read the first line in English like this "while not game done do the loop." The exclamation point (`!`) is very similar to the keyword `not`, which you used previously. I'm showing you the exclamation point version so you get used to seeing it.

5. The main part of the loop uses the game object to "run the game":

```
if game.get_high_number
   if game.get_guess_count
```

You're using a couple of different conditional `if` statements to first set up the game. The game object will ask the user for his choice of maximum high number and how many guesses he thinks he'll be able to guess in.

The methods will return true or false depending on whether they correctly got the player's input. If not, they'll fail and the game will start the round again until it gets good input from the player.

6. When the player has supplied the needed data, the game can run a round:

```
game.prepare_computer_number
while !game.round_done? do
  puts ""
  game.get_player_guess
  game.show_results
end
game.next_round
```

The game prepares its secret number, and then runs another loop while the guessing is going on, alternating between getting a guess, and showing the results. The cool thing is you can almost read that out loud and have it make sense.

Picking names for variables, objects, and methods is hard. Some say it's one of the hardest problems of computer science! Using names that are descriptive and mean something to you makes it so much easier to understand what's going on in your code.

7. Finally, finish up with the missing `end` statements and final game results method call:

```
        end
    end
end

puts ""
game.print_final_score
```

8. Save your code. Go ahead and try to run it. Ruby will let you know that something (actually multiple things) are missing (as shown in Figure 6-1).

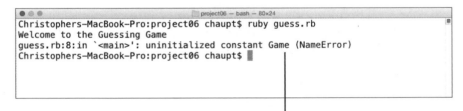

```
Christophers-MacBook-Pro:project06 chaupt$ ruby guess.rb
Welcome to the Guessing Game
guess.rb:8:in `<main>': uninitialized constant Game (NameError)
Christophers-MacBook-Pro:project06 chaupt$
```

Ruby guides you to the next piece of code that needs to be written.

Figure 6-1: Hmm, Ruby is wondering where our game is!

Creating Placeholder Classes

Again, you'll use Ruby to help you figure out what needs to be coded. You'll start with the basics and slowly fill them in. Because Ruby was complaining about not knowing what the `Game` class is, let's fix that first.

The actual message from Ruby said something about an "uninitialized constant Game" or something like that. You might have noticed that the word *game* started with a capital letter. You might also remember that I mentioned that Ruby programmers use capitals for constants. Well, class names turn out to be constants! Instead of using all capitals, the convention for class names is to capitalize each "word" in the name like this: VeryLongClassName.

Creating an empty Game class

First, I'll show you an empty class. Then you'll fill it in.

1. Ruby has a special keyword for identifying a class called, well, class. Add this code to the top of your file after the initial comments:

```
class Game
# Game class code goes here
end
```

2. If you saved and ran the code now, you'd notice that Ruby no longer warns you about missing the constant Game, but instead doesn't know about the TOTAL_ROUNDS constant. So, fix that by adding code below the comment above (all class code will go between the class line and the final end line.

```
TOTAL_ROUNDS = 3
```

3. Now if you run the code, you should get the welcome message using the number 3 for how many rounds the game will be played in. If you enter your name at the prompt, you get a new error about missing Player constants now that is similar to the prior message.

Creating an empty Player class

The process for creating the initial Player class is the same as you just did for Game:

1. Set up the empty class for a player:

```
class Player
  # Player class code goes here
end
```

2. Save and run. This time Ruby indicates that there is something wrong with `initialize` and the number of arguments it uses. What's that (see Figure 6-2)?

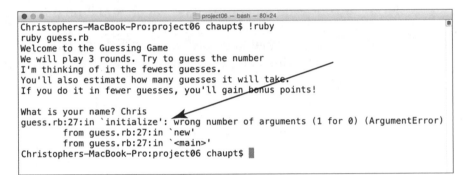

```
● ● ●                    project06 — bash — 80×24
Christophers-MacBook-Pro:project06 chaupt$ !ruby
ruby guess.rb
Welcome to the Guessing Game
We will play 3 rounds. Try to guess the number
I'm thinking of in the fewest guesses.
You'll also estimate how many guesses it will take.
If you do it in fewer guesses, you'll gain bonus points!

What is your name? Chris
guess.rb:27:in `initialize': wrong number of arguments (1 for 0) (ArgumentError)
        from guess.rb:27:in `new'
        from guess.rb:27:in `<main>'
Christophers-MacBook-Pro:project06 chaupt$ ▌
```

Figure 6-2: Wrong number of arguments? But what is initialize?

3. Add an initialize method inside of the `Player` class near its top:

```
def initialize(name)
  @name          = name
  @score         = 0
  prepare_for_new_round
end
```

You're going to set up some special variables called *instance* variables. The variables with the at sign (@) in front of them are instance variables. Here you have one for the name and one for the score of the player. You're assigning the passed in value for the player's name to the instance variable called @name. Instance variables are available to all other methods you will create in the `Player` object. Instance variables are *not* available to other code.

The `initialize` method is a method that Ruby calls every time you create a new object from a class using the `new` call. Remember when you created a new `Player` object in the main program and passed in the name? Doing that automatically called `initialize` for you. Ruby uses the `initialize` method for any setup that may be needed for your object. Every object has a built-in `initialize` method, but by default it takes zero arguments. That's why you got the error you saw earlier.

4. The `initialize` method uses one other method internally to set up some additional instance variables. Write that code below the `initialize` method:

```
def prepare_for_new_round
  @total_guess_count    = 0
  @high_number          = 0
  @current_guess        = 0
  @current_number_of_guesses = 0
end
```

These instance variables will track various pieces of data about the user. You could put these variables in the `initialize` method, but I'm breaking them out here because you'll want to reset the values each time the player enters a new round of the game.

5. If you save, test, and run your program again, you'll see that another `initialize` is missing, this time for the `Game` object, because you're passing the player object to its `new` method. Notice that the error will look like Figure 6-2, but the line numbers will have changed.

Adding the missing initialize to the Game class

To finish up this section, you'll want to add the initialization related methods into the `Game` class.

1. Near the top of the `Game` class, after your definition of the `TOTAL_ROUNDS` constant, add the following:

```
def initialize(player)
  @player = player
  @round = 0
  next_round
end
```

You're setting up instance variables in the `Game` class that will refer to the player object and the current round number. You also call an instance method to set up some other variables.

2. Complete variable setup with a `next_round` method:

```
def next_round
  @computers_number = 0
  @round_done = false
  @round += 1
  @player.prepare_for_new_round
end
```

This method initializes some variables to track the round and calls a method on the `player` object to set itself up.

Calling a method on another object is called *sending a message* to that object. So in this example, the `game` object is sending the `player` object the message `prepare_for_new_round` with no arguments (it doesn't take any). In this book, I use both "calling" and "sending a message" when referring to one object working with another.

That funny `@round += 1` is something new. It's a Ruby shortcut for adding 1 to the value being held by the instance variable `@round`. It could have been written as `@round = @round + 1`, but the way I've written it is shorter. Programmers like to do as little typing as possible!

3. Save and test your program. You should see that you got past all the setup, and now Ruby is telling you that it can't find the done? method on the game object at the start of the big while loop (see Figure 6-3). It's time to fill in the game's rules.

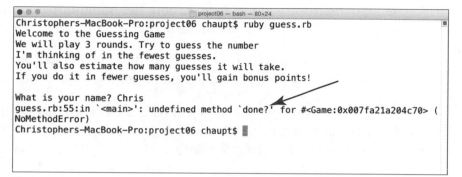

```
● ○ ○                    📄 project06 — bash — 80×24
Christophers-MacBook-Pro:project06 chaupt$ ruby guess.rb
Welcome to the Guessing Game
We will play 3 rounds. Try to guess the number
I'm thinking of in the fewest guesses.
You'll also estimate how many guesses it will take.
If you do it in fewer guesses, you'll gain bonus points!

What is your name? Chris
guess.rb:55:in `<main>': undefined method `done?' for #<Game:0x007fa21a204c70> (
NoMethodError)
Christophers-MacBook-Pro:project06 chaupt$ █
```

Figure 6-3: Setup is working now, but the start of the game loop needs work.

Adding Player Methods

Now that you're working with multiple objects, you have to decide what you're going to write code for first. In your previous project, you programmed the application "top down," writing the higher-level concepts first and slowly working your way down to the low-level stuff.

In the guessing game, you're doing a bit of both. You coded the main game loop and the rest of the skeleton of the game, as well as the more basic parts of the two classes you're using.

Now you'll work on filling out the Player class so any player object that is created will have the functionality needed by the Game class.

Creating player getter methods

Earlier I explained that when you create an object from a class in Ruby, any instance variables (the ones with the @) are hidden away inside the object. Without help, the outside world can't read or write to these variables.

Hidden variables sound like a bad thing, but they're actually really good. If the variable isn't visible to the outside of the object, it can't be accidentally (or intentionally) messed with and disturb your intentions. Programmers call this *information hiding* and talk about the *visibility* of variables. Good object-oriented program design looks for ways to expose only the minimum amount of data necessary in ways that are safe and under your control.

So how do you make variables available to code outside the object? You create a *getter* method to, um, get the data!

1. Getters are super easy — just return the variable. Do that for the player's name right after the `prepare_for_new_round` method in the `Player` class:

   ```
   def name
     @name
   end
   ```

2. Create a getter for the score:

   ```
   def score
     @score
   end
   ```

3. Create a getter for the total guess count:

   ```
   def total_guess_count
     @total_guess_count
   end
   ```

4. Create a getter for the player's high number choice:

   ```
   def high_number
     @high_number
   end
   ```

5. Create a getter for the current guess made by the player:

```
def current_guess
  @current_guess
end
```

6. Create a getter for the count of guesses in this round:

```
def guess_count
  @current_number_of_guesses
end
```

These methods look pretty simple, and they are. But they also serve the important purpose of requiring a programmer to send the right message to get the value she wants, and not access the instance variable directly.

Creating player setter methods

Setter methods do the opposite of getter methods. In this game, only one method is a setter.

The game can change the player's score at the end of the round, so write a method to permit this:

```
def add_score(points)
  @score += points
end
```

Why not call this set_score? You could, but I believe it's easier to understand the purpose of adding points to the current score if you call it add_score. Notice that you're using the shortcut += to add points to the current value of @score.

Adding player utility methods

A few methods are sort of getters, but are special, so I'm calling them _utility methods_. They do get values from the object, but in a special way as they read input from the keyboard.

Add the utility methods inside of the `Player` class :

1. Write a method that gets the highest number the player wants the game to use for the range of numbers to select a secret choice from:

```
def get_high_number
  @high_number = gets.to_i
end
```

You're using your old friend `gets` to read the player's input. The `to_i` method immediately converts the input to a number, stores it into the `@high_number` instance variable, and because this is the last line of the method, returns that to the code that called this method.

2. Create a similar method to get the player's best guess as to how many turns are going to be needed to figure out the game's secret number:

```
def get_total_guess_count
  @total_guess_count = gets.to_i
end
```

3. Create a helper method that will be used to get the player's current guess during each turn.

```
def get_guess
  @current_number_of_guesses += 1
  @current_guess = gets.to_i
end
```

Note how this also keeps track of how many guesses the player had made by adding one to the `@current_number_of_guesses` instance variable.

4. Save and run your code. Because you just wrote a bunch of low-level methods on the `Player` class, nothing should have changed. You really need to finish the `Game` class now.

Writing the Game Class Code

Now it's time to finish the Game class. There is a lot to do, so let's dive in.

Be sure to add all this code inside the Game class. You can start to add it right after the next_round method that should already be in there.

Coding the Game class getters

The Game class has a few getters that are used in the main program loop and inside the class itself. Add these methods:

1. Get the current round number:

```
def round
  @round
end
```

2. Return a Boolean value of true or false if the game is done:

```
def done?
  @round > TOTAL_ROUNDS
end
```

You don't have a full if statement there with the conditional check. Ruby will still figure out what's going on by comparing the value inside the @round instance variable with the constant TOTAL_ROUNDS. If the round number is larger than 3, the condition will return true; otherwise, it will return false.

3. Return whether the round is done:

```
def round_done?
  @round_done
end
```

The @round_done instance variable is what programmers call a *flag variable*. A flag is set in one part of the application to signal some other part that something happened. In the guessing game, the game object will set the variable to true when it detects that the round is done, and the code outside the object will be able to see that to end the round loop in the main code.

Setting up the round

Each round, the game will ask the player for some numbers it needs to run the game. The code should use the `player` object to retrieve inputs or other data from the player and check that the values make sense for the game.

1. Get the highest number that the game is permitted to use for the range in which to pick a secret number:

```
def get_high_number
  print "I'll pick a number between 1 and what
    number? "
  high_number = @player.get_high_number
  if high_number <= 1
    puts "Oops! The number must be larger than
    1. Try again."
    return false
  else
    return true
  end
end
```

This method has a lot of text in it, but basically it's prompting the player to pick a number. It uses a condition to make sure that the number is not less than or equal to one. That wouldn't make any sense! The method returns `true` if it worked properly and `false` if not. The main game loop uses that value to determine whether to continue to run the round. (Go back and read the main code if you need to. I'll wait.)

This is an example of using the keyword `return` explicitly. You don't need to do that, but it makes the code easier to read.

2. Get the guess count from the player. This is just a little bit of fun we're adding to the game to challenge the player to try to estimate how many guesses he'll need to figure out the secret number. If he can guess the number in fewer guesses, the game will give him bonus points.

```
def get_guess_count
  average = calculate_typical_number_of_guesses
  puts "How many guesses do you think it will
    take?"
  print "(average would be #{average}): "
  total_guess_count =
    @player.get_total_guess_count
  if total_guess_count < 1
    puts "Seriously #{@player.name}?! You need to
    at least try!"
    return false
  else
    return true
  end
end
```

I know this looks long, but it's printing a lot of text to the user to tell him what's going on. The code itself uses the same techniques you've already seen.

3. One method that get_guess_count uses is calculate_typical_number_of_guesses. Write that method now:

```
def calculate_typical_number_of_guesses
  typical_count = Math.sqrt(@player.high_number)
  typical_count.round
end
```

This method uses some complicated math to come up with a number for the typical number of guesses needed to pick a randomly selected secret number. Note that you're using the

Ruby Math libraries square root method (sqrt) and also the round method to make sure the number returned from this method is a whole number.

If you've studied algebra or heard of the binary search algorithm, you may see what's going on here. If you haven't, don't worry — it isn't important! Just know that we're using some math that estimates the number of tries needed if you used one of the best algorithms for searching for a number.

4. The last setup thing to do is to have the Game object pick a secret number:

```
def prepare_computer_number
    @computers_number = rand(@player.high_number)
    + 1
end
```

Remember that the rand method picks a random number between zero and one less than your number, so that's why you add one at the end.

5. You've been typing a lot! You aren't quite done, but be sure to save!

Running the guessing loop

With everything set up, the game needs code to actually run the guessing part of the game.

1. Get the player's guess for this turn:

```
def get_player_guess
  print "#{@player.name}, what is your guess? "
  @player.get_guess
  compare_player_guess_to_computer_number
end
```

2. After the player returns a guess, the game needs to see if the
player is correct or needs a hint:

```
def compare_player_guess_to_computer_number
  if @player.current_guess == @computers_number
    @round_done = true
    puts "YEAH!!!!! You guessed it!"
    calculate_score
  else
    show_hint
  end
end
```

If the player's current guess is the same as the secret number
selected by the Game object, then the player is done with the
round. This is where you mark the flag variable @round_done.
You also can calculate the score for the round. If the player
didn't guess the number, give him a hint.

Adding the hint code

This guessing game is a little devious in that it doesn't *always* tell
the truth!

1. Prepare a hint message depending on whether the player's
choice is higher or lower than the game's secret number:

```
def show_hint
  hints = ["low", "high"]
  if @player.current_guess < @computers_number
    hint_index = 0
  else
    hint_index = 1
  end
  if !tell_truth?
    hint_index = hint_index - 1
    hint_index = hint_index.abs
  end
  puts "HINT: You are too #{hints[hint_index]}"
end
```

This method uses a few interesting techniques. First, it stores the low or high hint words in an array. Then it tries to figure out which word it should use by testing a conditional comparing the player's guess with the computer's number. If the player is too low, you set a variable to zero; otherwise, you set it to one. Those numbers are the *index* into the array for the word you want to use. The syntax `hints[hint_index]` is how you refer to the correct item.

Recall in earlier projects where I described an array as a chain of boxes or series of compartments, which I'll call *slots*. Each slot is numbered, starting with the first slot, which is number zero. Yes programmers are funny and like to start at zero when counting! In the hint method, you're using the `hint_index` local variable to point to the correct box, depending on the condition.

2. Create a method that randomly decides whether to tell the truth:

```
def tell_truth?
   rand(100) >= 4
end
```

`rand` will pick a number between 0 and 99. If the number is greater than or equal to four, the condition will be true and the hint method will "tell the truth."

The math in the truth-telling condition in `show_hint` is a little tricky. It's subtracting one from the current value, and then taking the absolute value of that number. This changes a current value of 1 to 0, and changes 0 to –1 (whose absolute value is 1). It flips the result!

Scoring the round

Scoring the round is pretty simple in comparison:

```
def calculate_score
  score = 0
  if @player.guess_count > @player.total_guess_count
    score = 1
  elsif @player.total_guess_count <
    calculate_typical_number_of_guesses
    score = 3
  else
    score = 5
  end
  @player.add_score(score)
end
```

If the player took more turns then he originally thought he would, he gets one point. If he took less than the number of turns he thought he would need, he gets three points. If he is exactly right, he gets the most points (five) because that is pretty amazing.

Note how you're using the player setter to add the round's score to the player's overall score.

Showing the player the results

Finally, you need a couple of help methods that display the results of each turn and the overall game.

1. Display the current status of the turn during a round:

```
def show_results
  puts "Guess count: #{@player.guess_count}
    target: #{@player.total_guess_count}"
end
```

Nothing too special here. Just printing out some of the player's numbers.

2. Show the final score for the game:

```
def print_final_score
  puts "Final score for #{@player.name} is
    #{@player.score}"
end
```

3. Save, test, and run the game. It should run and look like Figure 6-4.

```
● ● ●                    📁 project06 — bash — 80×24
Chris, what is your guess? 3
YEAH!!!!! You guessed it!
Guess count: 2 target: 4

------> Round #3

I'll pick a number between 1 and what number? 10
How many guesses do you think it will take?
(average would be 3): 4

Chris, what is your guess? 5
HINT: You are too low
Guess count: 1 target: 4

Chris, what is your guess? 7
HINT: You are too high
Guess count: 2 target: 4

Chris, what is your guess? 6
YEAH!!!!! You guessed it!
Guess count: 3 target: 4

Final score for Chris is 15
Christophers-MacBook-Pro:project06 chaupt$ ▋
```

Figure 6-4: The final game in progress.

Trying Some Experiments

This project has a lot of code, but it introduces a number of new concepts. The most important is that of classes. I only used the most basic functionality to split the game into three parts: the main code, the `Player` object, and the `Game` object. In future projects, I'll break things down even more and show you more of Ruby's built-in classes and objects.

There are a lot of things you could do with this game. Why not try a few?

✔ If the game is dragging on too long, it would be nice if the player could quit without having to press Ctrl+C. Can you figure out how to add a quit feature?

✔ Add some additional statistics like the total number of guesses across all rounds.

✔ Change the scoring to be based on the number of guesses in total. If the player picks a number that is a lot higher than the average calculated number of guesses needed, he may get penalized.

✔ Change the hints algorithm to tell the player if he's getting hotter or colder based on how close or far his guess is from the actual secret number.

✔ What is the impact of the "lying" feature of the game? Does it make the game more or less fun that the computer isn't always telling the truth? How would you change this?

Part III
Working with Lots of Your Own Data

```
● ● ●                    📁 project08 — bash — 80×24
Christophers-MacBook-Pro:project08 chaupt$ ruby codebreak.rb
Code Breaker will encrypt or decrypt a file of your choice

Do you want to (e)ncrypt or (d)ecrypt a file? d
Enter the name of the input file: secret.txt
Enter the name of the output file: final.txt
Enter the secret password: brutus
All done!
Christophers-MacBook-Pro:project08 chaupt$ cat final.txt
Friends, Romans, countrymen, lend me your ears;
I come to bury Caesar, not to praise him.
The evil that men do lives after them;
The good is oft interred with their bones;
So let it be with Caesar. The noble Brutus
Hath told you Caesar was ambitious:
If it were so, it was a grievous fault,
And grievously hath Caesar answer'd it.
Here, under leave of Brutus and the rest--
For Brutus is an honourable man;
So are they all, all honourable men--

Antony
Christophers-MacBook-Pro:project08 chaupt$ ▉
```

In this part . . .

 For tips on organizing your Ruby code, go to
www.dummies.com/extras/rubyforkids.

Short Straw

Sometimes when you have a group of people, you need
to randomly select one of them to do something. Maybe that's
to go first in a game, to do a chore, or just for fun you want to
see who is the last person standing (think musical chairs). One
old game that's sometimes used to pick somebody is to take a
bundle of straws (or sticks or pencils), make them all the same
size except for one of them, and then randomly pick from the
bundle. Whoever gets the short straw is "out" (or wins, depending on how you look at it!).

This project is going to dive a little more deeply into the `Array`
object you've been using in some of the prior projects. Up until
now, I've just used it with some basic functionality, but here,
you'll see that it's a pretty powerful tool. I'll show you a few
different ways to use arrays, and as a bonus, I'll show you a few
shortcuts you can use when working with arrays and classes.

```
● ● ●                    project07 — bash — 80×24
Christophers-MacBook-Pro:project07 chaupt$ ruby straws.rb
Welcome to the Last Straw Game
In each round, players will draw straws of two different lengths.
The players who pick the short straw will be eliminated and
a new round will begin.

-----> Round 1

=================== anne
=================== bert
=================== chris
=================== donna
=================== ernie
=================== franz
=================== garfield
=================== holden
================= ivy
===== jose

-----> Round 2

=================== anne
===== bert
=================== chris
```

Organizing a New Project

You'll use Atom to create and edit your program. You'll store this project in a single Ruby file. And you'll use the terminal program to run, test, and play around with the short straw code.

If you haven't created a `development` folder already, refer to Project 2 for information on how to do that.

1. Start your terminal program and enter the development folder:

   ```
   $ cd development
   ```

2. Create a new directory for this project:

   ```
   $ mkdir project07
   ```

3. Move into the new directory:

   ```
   $ cd project07
   ```

4. Start Atom by double-clicking its icon.

5. Create a new source code file by choosing File ➪ New File.

6. Save it by choosing File ➪ Save and store it in your `project07` directory. Call the file `straws.rb`.

If some of these steps are confusing to you, refer to the "Organizing a New Project" section in Project 4. It provides more details for each step.

You're now ready to dive into arrays some more and build an elimination-round, tournament-style straw drawing game.

Planning the Project

In theory, this project is much simpler than prior projects, at least with respect to the idea of a bunch of people taking a random straw, and then seeing who picked the "short" one. Don't let this simplicity fool you, though! You still want to plan out the overall approach to the code, and as you write out the Ruby, I'll take a little time to show you that there is more than one way to do many of the same logical steps. You'll see that Ruby provides a number of tools that make it easier to write less code.

I have this saying that programmer's are lazy. Do I mean that they don't like to do their chores? Well, no, not usually. I mean that the best code ever written is the code you never write! What?!? The more lines of code you write, the more opportunities there are to create bugs and other problems. To become an expert programmer, you'll look for ways to use other people's code (such as the built-in methods, objects, and classes that Ruby provides), and you'll look for techniques that allow you to write fewer lines of code yet get the same amount of work done. I'll show you a few in this project.

There will be a game object that manages a group of players (also objects) and runs rounds of the game. Each round, the players will be given new straws (yet additional objects) to compare against one another. The game object is also where the rules of the game are coded, even for such a simple game.

The game should welcome the players and provide a short introduction of what's going to happen.

Unlike prior projects, you won't have to enter a bunch of players at the start of the game. Instead, you'll provide an array of names, and the game object will use that to generate a set of associated player objects.

Each round, the game will create a new "bundle" (really just another array) of straw objects. It will count how many players remain in the game, and generate one straw for each of those players. The game will make one of the straws "shorter" than the others.

The game will assign one straw to each player. It'll print out a message that shows what round is being played. It'll also print out all remaining players so you can see which player has which kind of straw. The game will remove the player with the short straw from the remaining players (how sad!). If the game determines that there is more than one player remaining, it will run another round. When only one player remains, the game ends and displays the winner.

This is a simple game, but it gives you a chance to try a few different techniques for working with arrays. Ruby arrays are one of the core data structures you'll use all the time in your own programs, so it's worth getting familiar with all the tools Ruby gives you.

Data structure is a fancy term that refers to how you organize and work with your information. It might be something as simple as a plain number or string (often called a *primitive* or *primitive data structure*), or it might be something slightly more complicated like a container such as an array or a hash (which we haven't used yet). You may not know it, but you've been creating your own data structures as you've implemented classes for objects like Player or Game in these projects. A data structure can be thought of as an abstract type of information (so I talk about Player objects, and know that a player is made up of a name, and a straw in this project).

Looking at the Program Skeleton

You'll continue to use what you've learned about object-oriented programming and sketch out this project in the form of several classes and a main program to use them. You'll need to create a Player, Straw, and Game set of classes and a little bit of Ruby to get everything started.

1. Switch over to Atom and your `straws.rb` file. Enter a comment at the top that provides a little information about the project:

```
#
# Ruby For Kids Project 7: Straws
# Programmed By: Chris Haupt
# Elimination-round, tournament-style, avoid the
    shortest straw, or else!
#
```

2. Be kind to your users and provide a short introduction to let them know what's about to happen:

```
puts "Welcome to the Last Straw Game"
puts "In each round, players will draw straws of
    two different lengths."
puts "The players who pick the short straw will be
    eliminated and"
puts "a new round will begin."
```

3. Unlike earlier projects, you'll skip the data entry required when requesting player names, and instead just build an array of names to use. Feel free to make these names anything you want and assign them to the constant called PLAYERS:

```
PLAYERS = %w(anne bert chris donna ernie franz
    garfield holden ivy jose)
```

 Wait a second! That is an odd-looking array. Remember how I told you I was going to show a few Ruby shortcuts? Here is the first one. The little `%w` symbol means to create an array where the strings are separated by white space. You can absolutely write this array the long way like this:

```
PLAYERS = ["anne", "bert", "chris", "donna",
    "ernie", "franz", "garfield", "holden", "ivy",
    "jose"]
```

Doing so requires three extra characters to be typed for each name (two quotes and one comma, except for the last name). Why do all that extra typing if there is a shortcut? Sometimes you have to use the longer form — for instance, if your name is Chris von Programmer, the white space in the name would confuse Ruby and it would break up the name incorrectly.

4. Create a new `Game` object by sending the `Game` class the `new` message and passing the `PLAYERS` array as its argument:

```
game = Game.new(PLAYERS)
```

5. You'll create a number of methods in the `Game` class to run the game. For now, write out the main game loop as if those methods already exist:

```
while !game.done? do
  game.show_round_number
  game.play_round
  game.show_results
  game.finish_round
end
```

The sequence of events here pretty much follows what you planned out earlier. By naming methods appropriately, you'll find that reading the code is super easy.

I mentioned this before, but naming is really important! Pick variable, method, and class names that are meaningful to you and to future readers of your code. *You* may be that future reader. When you come back and look at your program in six months, you'll be a lot happier that you sent your future self some easy-to-read code.

6. Finish the main part of the program by sending the `Game` object a message to display the winner of the short straw tournament:

```
game.show_winner
```

7. Save your code now. Switch on over to the terminal and run it.

```
$ ruby straws.rb
```

As expected, Ruby lets you know that the program isn't finished yet (see Figure 7-1).

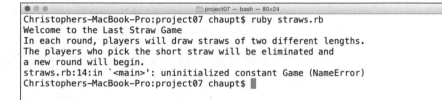

```
Christophers-MacBook-Pro:project07 chaupt$ ruby straws.rb
Welcome to the Last Straw Game
In each round, players will draw straws of two different lengths.
The players who pick the short straw will be eliminated and
a new round will begin.
straws.rb:14:in `<main>': uninitialized constant Game (NameError)
Christophers-MacBook-Pro:project07 chaupt$
```

Figure 7-1: Yup, time to start writing some classes.

Creating Placeholder Classes

As you learned in the previous project, you can use Ruby to guide you while writing your code. If you add some small bits of Ruby, save, and then run, the various warning and error messages Ruby produces give you a pretty good idea whether you're on track. I'll use that technique again here to help you get comfortable with it.

Creating an empty Game class

I'm going to show you the details of this program from the bottom up, but let's get some placeholders in the file first:

1. Type the empty Game class to start. Put it at the top of the straws.rb file, just below your comment:

```
class Game
    def initialize(player_names)
    end
# the rest of the game class code will go here
end
```

2. Because you already wrote the main program's implementation that uses this class, stub in the methods that it calls next.

The term *stub* is used by programmers to indicate a placeholder, temporary, or test implementation of some code. Here you're writing the methods that make your programming interface for the Game class but not (yet) filling in the code that actually *does* anything.

Write the method that indicates if the game is done. Put the code inside the Game class:

```
def done?
end
```

3. Write the method that will display the round's number:

```
def show_round_number
end
```

4. Write the method to play a round:

```
def play_round
end
```

5. Write the method to show the round's results:

```
def show_results
end
```

6. Write the method to complete the round and do any final bookkeeping:

```
def finish_round
end
```

7. Write the method to display who won the match:

```
def show_winner
end
```

8. Save your code and run it. You should see the introduction message, and then the program just sits there. If you recall, you have a `while` loop that is waiting for the Game object to indicate that it's done. That never happens, so you're in an infinite loop. Press Ctrl+C to get out (see Figure 7-2).

```
● ● ●                    project07 — bash — 80×24
Christophers-MacBook-Pro:project07 chaupt$ ruby straws.rb
Welcome to the Last Straw Game
In each round, players will draw straws of two different lengths.
The players who pick the short straw will be eliminated and
a new round will begin.
^Cstraws.rb:in `show_round_number': Interrupt
        from straws.rb:39:in `<main>'

Christophers-MacBook-Pro:project07 chaupt$ ▌
```

Figure 7-2: There are no immediate errors, but you're stuck in a loop.

Creating an empty Player class

Next up is the `Player` class, which will be used to store a player's name and current straw.

1. Add the empty `Player` class first and an initialization method to accept a name. Put this code above the `Game` class and below the top comment in the `straws.rb` file:

```
class Player
    def initialize(name)
      @name  = name
    end
    # the rest of the player code will go here
end
```

2. Save the code again. You can run it, too, to see if Ruby detects any other errors, but otherwise, you're still going to be stuck in that loop.

Creating an empty Straw class

You're going to represent the straws that players get with an object as well. The `Straw` class will keep track of the size of the straw (as a number) and be able to tell if it's the "short straw." Eventually, it will be able to draw itself, too.

1. Create a new class and add an initializer that accepts the size of the straw. Put this code above the `Player` class and below the top comment in the `straws.rb` file:

```ruby
class Straw
    def initialize(size)
     @straw_size = size
    end
    # the rest of the straw code will go here
end
```

2. Add some constants that you'll use to represent two different sizes of straws. The numbers don't matter much:

```ruby
SHORT_STRAW = 5
LONG_STRAW  = 20
```

Put this code right above the initialize method. In most cases the position doesn't matter, but I like putting things like constants at the top of the class to make it easier to find and see them.

3. Save again. Go ahead and run Ruby to look for any typos. Press Ctrl+C to escape the loop.

Coding the Straw Methods

I'm going to explain the short straw code in a bottom-up fashion for the rest of this project. As you fill out the classes, you'll begin to see that there are different ways to do things in Ruby, and I'll point out a few.

The purpose of the `Straw` class is to represent an object that knows how big it is and is able to display itself, and that's about it. Pretty simple. Simple objects are important, because it can make code easier to understand, easier to reuse, and easier to debug.

It's also a good idea to put code that is logically related together when possible. On the other hand, it's also a good idea to separate out pieces of code that have different jobs or responsibilities. We could have just built in the `Straw` capability directly into the `Player` class, but we're breaking it out because it's a different *thing*.

Creating straw getter methods

There are a couple of different pieces of information that need to be shared by a straw: whether it's short and what it looks like.

1. Create a method that can be used to test whether the straw is short:

   ```
   def short?
     @straw_size == SHORT_STRAW
   end
   ```

   This method will return a Boolean (a `true` or `false`) value. If the size of the straw is equal to your constant, it will return `true`. Otherwise, the straw will not be considered short and the method will return `false`.

2. Return some kind of string that represents what the straw looks like. You're still building a program that runs in a terminal window, but why not give the user something to look at other than just a number?

```
def appearance
  '=' * @straw_size
end
```

Pretty simple so far.

Creating the straw factory method

For this program, the main game object will run multiple rounds, each time reducing the number of players by one. On each of those rounds, the game also needs to construct another collection of straws for the players to use. To make this easier, you'll create a factory method that builds all the straw objects you need in one shot.

Programmers usually use the term *factory* to mean a method that builds other objects for you. Just like a real-world factory, you'll give the factory method an order (in this case, the number of straws you want), and it'll build the object(s) for you. In this program, the factory will create an array of Straw objects.

1. The straw factory will create an array of Straw objects. Let's call that array of straws a "bundle" just for fun and start writing the method like this:

```
def self.create_bundle(short, long)
```

This *almost* looks like a regular method. The name is fine — create_bundle tells us what the factory is going to build. The arguments are the number of short and long straws we want built. The self. part tells Ruby that this is a class method.

What is a class method? All the methods you have created so far didn't have that `self.` part in front of the method name. Remember that a method is a message that you send to a related object. But that assumes that the object exists already. How do you send a message when the object doesn't exist? One way is to send a message to the class itself. For the purposes of a factory method, you want to create new objects of a particular type, so you attach the method to the desired class using the `self.` syntax. You can then use the code to create any number of objects. You'll see this pattern often in Ruby for methods that are used to create or manipulate groups of objects.

2. Define an empty array for the bundle:

```
bundle = []
```

3. Now fill the array with new `Straw` objects:

```
1.upto(short) do
  bundle << Straw.new(SHORT_STRAW)
end
```

You've created a loop that will go as many times as the count inside the `short` variable. The `<<` syntax is one way to add an object to an array. Here you're creating a new `Straw` object, setting its size to the value in the `SHORT_STRAW` constant, and then adding that object to the array.

4. Write another loop for the long straws using the exact same technique:

```
1.upto(long) do
  bundle << Straw.new(LONG_STRAW)
end
```

You're adding the long straws to the end of the existing array.

5. Return the value that is held by the `bundle` variable and end the method. What do you think is the total length of the bundle?

```
    bundle
end
```

6. Save your code and run a quick test. You shouldn't see any errors, but nothing else will happen yet either.

An array primer

Arrays are one of the most basic and most useful container data structures you'll use when programming. Arrays are like boxes with many compartments or slots in which you can put things. An array of straws might look something like Figure 7-3.

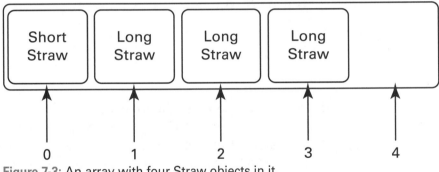

Figure 7-3: An array with four Straw objects in it.

Each slot holds one object. The slots are numbered starting at zero. In Figure 7-3, the first slot holds a short straw, and its number is zero. Programmers call the position number of an item in an array its *index number*.

In the previous section, the `create_bundle` factory method added new straws to the end of the array with the `<<` method. In Figure 7-3, if you were going to add another object at the end, it would go at index four.

Arrays in Ruby aren't a fixed size. The illustration here shows a box of a certain size, but in reality, the only limitation is the amount of memory available for Ruby to use. You can create some massive arrays if you need to.

Objects in an array are *randomly* accessible by referring to the index number of the object you want. For instance, in Figure 7-3, if you wanted to access the short straw, and the array was in the variable named `bundle`, you would use the syntax `bundle[0]`. If you wanted to get to the second item, that would be `bundle[1]`, and so on.

As you'll see throughout this project and others, there are a large number of helpful methods available to you to work with arrays.

Coding the Player Methods

The player object in this project is pretty simplistic and is composed of some getters and setters and a couple of helper methods.

Creating player getters and setters

The only data that the `Player` class is concerned with in this project is a name and its current `Straw` object.

1. Create a name getter. Up until now, you would write this like so:

   ```
   def name
     @name
   end
   ```

   This is a super simple method that just returns the value of the `@name` instance variable. Writing methods like this is extremely common, so Ruby gives you a shortcut that can be written in one line:

```
attr_reader :name
```

Behind the scenes, Ruby basically writes the same code as the first version. You get the same behavior but save some possible keystrokes.

What does the `attr` stand for? Programmers have a special name for instance variables of an object, particularly if they're exposed to the outside world. In Ruby, these are called *attributes*. Some programmers also call these *properties*. The call above is an attribute reader, which is another way to say a getter.

2. You need both a getter and setter to read and write the player's current `Straw` object. Use the short attribute access methods that Ruby provides:

```
attr_reader :straw
attr_writer :straw
```

Huh, that seems like too much typing, right? Well, Ruby has shorter shorthand for this common case, so use that instead:

```
attr_accessor :straw
```

Accessor is just a fancy way of saying "getter and setter rolled into one." Perhaps that isn't fancy, but it is less of a mouthful! Note that there is an interesting implication with using accessors. Access to attributes is available both to code outside the associated object and inside the object. You'll notice in future code that I'm not always using the instance variable directly (the @ is missing). When you see that, it means I'm using the attribute reader (or writer) instead.

It is very important that the *name of the accessor* (the part after the colon [:]) is exactly the same as the *instance variable name* (without the @). In the code you're writing, when I show an accessor, I'm also sometimes using the instance variable. This is almost always with the `initialize` method to set up the variable. If the names were spelled differently, then they wouldn't be referring to the same value and you would have a hard to find bug to track down! For instance, `@name` and `:name` are the same other than the leading symbol, so they're okay.

Creating player helper methods

The game requires a couple of helpers when working with `Player` objects, so write those now:

1. For the user interface of this project, you'll just want to display the straw appearance alongside the player's name. Use string interpolation to build this up:

    ```
    def appearance
      "#{straw.appearance} #{name}"
    end
    ```

2. The game loop is going to need to see if a player is holding the short straw, so provide a method to test this:

    ```
    def short_straw?
      straw.short?
    end
    ```

    This is a simple little method that lets the game engine deal with just testing the player object to see if it's holding a short straw. The game engine *could* reach in and check the straw by getting it from the player first, but that isn't a good programming approach. Using a method on the player instead hides the details of figuring out what the player is holding and whether it qualifies as "short."

3. Save the code before moving on to the game object work.

Coding Game Methods

It's time to finish the project and make use of the other objects you've just written. For each of these tasks, create or update the associated method inside the Game class.

Code initialization and the end condition

Move over to the Game class to start updating the stubbed methods there.

1. Enter the full implementation of the initialization code. It will be used to generate a set of player objects using the supplied name array:

```
def initialize(player_names)
  @players = []
    player_names.each do |name|
    @players.push(Player.new(name))
  end
  @rounds  = 1
end
```

You're also starting the round count at one, and you'll use that for the user interface.

This setup code looks pretty familiar to what you did in the create_bundle factory method in Straw, doesn't it? You're loading an array with Player objects in this case, but I'm using a different method called push, rather than <<. The push method appends the object at the end of the array and is nearly identical to <<. I want to illustrate that there is often more than one way to do something in Ruby. If you carefully look at the Ruby documentation, you may spot some differences, but they aren't important here. You should use the method that is easier for you to understand.

2. Update the done? method to provide a real result:

```
def done?
  @players.length <= 1
end
```

The test you're using here is to see if there is more than one player object in the array in the @players instance variable. Every round will be removing at least one object, so eventually this condition should be true.

Code user interface methods

The user interface for the project will display the current round number, the results of the round, and the final winner's name.

1. Using your basic string output knowledge, create a simple round indicator:

```
def show_round_number
  puts ""
  puts "----> Round #{@rounds}"
  puts ""
end
```

2. Using the player classes ability to generate an appearance for the player, display the results of drawing straws for all players in the current round:

```
def show_results
  @players.each do |player|
    puts player.appearance
  end
end
```

The each method loops through the array in the @players instance variable. In each cycle, it puts the next player object in the player local variable and then does whatever is in the block of code between the do and the associated end keyword. This is probably the most common way to loop through an array.

3. The winner of the game is represented by the last object in the @players array.

```
def show_winner
  last_player = @players.first
  puts ""
  puts "The winner is #{last_player.name}"
  puts ""
end
```

Ruby's array class gives you a nice method called first that returns the first element in the array. In your code, there should only ever be one remaining player at the end of the game. Remember from the array discussion earlier in this chapter that you can refer to objects in an array by their index numbers. You could have wrote the last_player assignment line like this:

```
last_player = @players[0]
```

I think using the first method is a little easier to read, but that's a matter of personal preference.

Coding the main game logic methods

We're in the home stretch, but we still need to implement the basic game logic methods, so let's do that now.

1. The `play_round` method does the work of preparing the straws for the round and passing them out to the players:

```
def play_round
  bundle_of_straws = setup_new_bundle
  0.upto(@players.length - 1) do |index|
    player = @players[index]
    player.straw = bundle_of_straws.pop
  end
end
```

Notice that I'm showing you yet another way to loop through an array. You may think this is a little more complicated looking than using the `each` method, and you're right. However, let's look at what's going on. I'm using the trusty `upto` method to count from zero to the length of the player array minus one. Why is that? I'm trying to generate the index numbers for the array. Remember, these start at the number zero for the first item. If I didn't take away one at the end, I'd be trying to get one too many items from the array. Ruby doesn't like that! Inside of the loop, I get the current number in the `index` variable and use the array index access method (the square brackets: `@players[index]`) to get the next player.

One new array method being used here is the `pop` method. The `pop` method removes the last item on the array and returns that. The `bundle_of_straws` local variable contains a randomly sorted array of `Straw` objects. The code grabs the last one off the array and assigns it to the player using the straw setter (accessor) of the player object. Phew! That's a lot of words for a few short lines of code.

2. The `play_round` method uses the `setup_new_bundle` method that we haven't created yet, so you'll write that next:

```
def setup_new_bundle
  number_of_players = @players.length
  bundle = Straw.create_bundle(1, number_of_
    players - 1)
  bundle.shuffle
end
```

This method first determines how many players there are. The array object provides the `length` method to return the total number of items in the array. Next, you use the handy factory method from the `Straw` class to create a new array of `Straw` objects. In this game, you're going to create one short straw, and the rest will be long straws. Finally, the Ruby array class provides a nice utility method for randomly mixing up the items in the array, much as you would shuffle a deck of cards. You use `shuffle`, and the mixed-up array is returned as the result of the method.

3. Finally, code the Ruby to complete a round of the game:

```
def finish_round
  @players.delete_if do |player|
    player.short_straw?
  end
  @rounds += 1
end
```

Here is *another* method provided to you by Ruby's array class: `delete_if`. This is a special kind of loop. What `delete_if` does is loop through the contents of the array, passing each item to the block of code using the `player` local variable. Inside of the block of code, you call the player's `short_straw?` method to check to see if that player has the short straw. If the value is `true`, then that tells the `delete_if` method to remove that object from the array. How handy!

4. Save the code and run the project. You should get a lot of output showing the progress of the game and then a final winner just like in Figure 7-4. Try running the program a few times and you'll see different results.

```
● ● ●                    project07 — bash — 80×24
===== garfield
==================== holden

----> Round 7

===== donna
==================== ernie
==================== franz
==================== holden

----> Round 8

==================== ernie
==================== franz
===== holden

----> Round 9

==================== ernie
===== franz

The winner is ernie

Christophers-MacBook-Pro:project07 chaupt$
```

Figure 7-4: The final output should show a winner!

Trying Some Experiments

Although this project is a rather simple idea, it shows you the power of using Ruby's array class, one of the most common data structures you're likely to use when programming.

You could do more things with this project. Why not try a few?

✔ What happens if you change the composition of the bundle of straws? Try having more than one short straw.

✔ What happens if you don't shuffle the straws?

✔ Using techniques you learned in the previous project, try adding the ability to type in names of players instead of starting with a hard-coded list.

✔ I didn't use `attr_accessor` in the `Game` class. Could I have? Try it out.

✔ Come up with some other ways to implement the user interface.

Code Breaker

Welcome to the world of encryption, ciphers, and secret messages! Have you ever wanted to send someone a hidden message that only you and the person you're sending it to could understand? Maybe you came up with a secret code on your own and used it to manually translate a letter or note — but that can be a lot of work. Converting messages into a form that hides their meaning is called *encryption,* and converting the message back to something that is easy to understand is called *decryption.* Why not let a computer do that work for you?

In this project, you write a Ruby program that will do the labor-intensive work of encrypting and decrypting your notes. You'll be able to write your note in your editor and save it as a file. Then you'll be able to use the project's program to convert the note into a hard-to-read, encrypted form. The same program will be able to take an encrypted file and change it back to something you can read.

```
● ● ●                    📁 project08 — bash — 80×24
Christophers-MacBook-Pro:project08 chaupt$ ruby codebreak.rb
Code Breaker will encrypt or decrypt a file of your choice

Do you want to (e)ncrypt or (d)ecrypt a file? d
Enter the name of the input file: secret.txt
Enter the name of the output file: final_message.txt
Enter the secret password: brutus
All done!
Christophers-MacBook-Pro:project08 chaupt$ cat secret.txt
Lxoktjy, Xusgty, iuAtzxEskt, rktj sk EuAx kgxy;
O iusk zu hAxE Igkygx, tuz zu vxgoyk nos.
Znk kBor zngz skt ju roBky glzkx znks;
Znk muuj oy ulz otzkxxkj Cozn znkox hutky;
Yu rkz oz hk Cozn Igkygx. Znk tuhrk HxAzAy
Ngzn zurj EuA Igkygx Cgy gshozouAy:
Ol oz Ckxk yu, oz Cgy g mxokBuAy lgArz,
Gtj mxokBuAyrE ngzn Igkygx gtyCkx'j oz.
Nkxk, Atjkx rkgBk ul HxAzAy gtj znk xkyz--
Lux HxAzAy oy gt nutuAxghrk sgt;
Yu gxk znkE grr, grr nutuAxghrk skt--

GtzutE
Christophers-MacBook-Pro:project08 chaupt$ █
```

Organizing a New Project

In this project, you use Atom to create and edit your program and to create test files with secret messages. You store this project's source code in a single Ruby file. The secret messages are stored in other files. You use the terminal program to run, test, and play around with the project code.

If you haven't created a `development` folder already, refer to Project 2 for information on how to do that.

1. Start your terminal program and enter the `development` folder:

   ```
   $ cd development
   ```

2. Create a new directory for this project:

   ```
   $ mkdir project08
   ```

3. Move in to the new directory:

   ```
   $ cd project08
   ```

4. Start Atom by double-clicking its icon.

5. Create a new source code file by choosing File ➪ New File. Save it by choosing File ➪ Save and store it in your `project08` directory. Call the file `codebreaker.rb`.

If some of these steps are confusing to you, refer to the "Organizing a New Project" section from Project 4. It provides more details for each step.

Planning the Project

The challenge of keeping messages secret has been around for a very long time. In fact, the relatively simple technique I'm going to show you in this project was used thousands of years ago by the likes of Julius Caesar! If you've ever written out coded message by hand, you may have even used the Caesar cipher that you'll program here.

Even though the overall Ruby program will be short, let's plan out what the program will do. A main object manages the Code Breaker user interface and input and output of files to be encrypted and decrypted. You'll put all the code to do the work of running the program in here. Unlike past programs, very little code will be outside of classes, only the smallest bit necessary to start up the program.

A second object contains the code for the encryption process itself. By breaking this object out into its own class, you'll be able to easily swap in other algorithms if you want to explore encryption a bit more. In fact, I'll challenge you at the end of the chapter to find a second way to use Ruby to implement the Caesar cipher.

The project's version of the Caesar cipher will use a technique called a lookup table, which basically will be nearly identical to how you would use the cipher if you were using paper and pencil. I'll show you a new data structure called a *hash,* which after arrays, I consider to be one of the most useful built-in data structures that Ruby provides.

I'll provide a lot of little details as I show you how to write the two classes for this program. The techniques you'll use to read and write files will prove useful in the future when you need to work with a lot of data. The new data structure that you'll use will also come into play frequently in future projects.

Seeing how the Caesar cipher works

Historians tell us that Julius Caesar used his *cipher* (secret code) to protect important military and political messages more than 2,000 years ago. Although other forms of encryption are known to have been used even before that time, the Caesar cipher is a good one to start with because it's relatively easy to understand.

This code is known as a *shift cipher* or *substitution cipher.* In it, you take each letter of your message and change it to another letter following a specific pattern. Caesar's original pattern was to take the alphabet and shift it by three letters to the left. For instance, the letter *J* would change to the letter *G.* For letters near the start of the alphabet, you would rotate around to the other end of the alphabet, so the letter *C* would become the letter *Z.* See Figure 8-1 for an example:

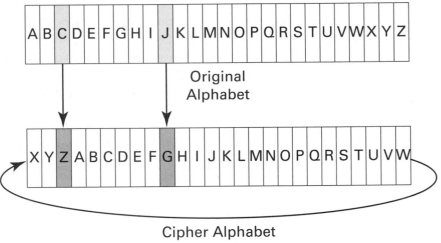

Figure 8-1: The regular alphabet lines up with the rotated one.

If you line up the original alphabet with the rotated one, you can quickly look up the original letter and find the encoded one right below it (as in Figure 8-1). To decode your message, as long as you know how many spaces the alphabet was rotated, you can reverse the process. Just pick the letter on the cipher alphabet, and then look up the actual letter in the regular alphabet. Easy!

Looking at the program skeleton

As you grow your coding skills, you'll begin to learn ways that you can write your code so that it's easier to understand and maintain. With object-oriented programming languages like Ruby, one such technique is to wrap as much functionality into reusable classes as possible. The code breaker project is pretty simple — you'll place almost all the code into one of two classes. However, you also need a small bit of code that will be used to start up the whole program.

1. Like with your previous projects, place some kind of comment at the top of the `codebreak.rb` file that describes what it's all about:

   ```
   #
   # Ruby For Kids Project 8: Code Breaker
   # Programmed By: Chris Haupt
   # A program that will encrypt and decrypt another
       document using the Caesar cipher
   #
   ```

2. Add a simple welcome message that will be displayed for the user:

   ```
   puts "Code Breaker will encrypt or decrypt a file
       of your choice"
   puts ""
   ```

3. Create a new object by creating an instance of the main project class:

   ```
   codebreaker = CodeBreaker.new
   ```

Programmers call the process of creating a new object *instantiation;* the object is called an *instance* of the associated class. In Ruby, when you send a class the `new` message, it calls your `initialize` method if you supplied one and returns the new object ready for you to use.

4. The CodeBreaker class will do all the work of running the program, including handling all the user interface needed to interact with the program's user. Create a condition that displays a message depending upon whether the codebreaker object did or did not work properly:

```
if codebreaker.run
  puts "All done!"
else
  puts "Didn't work!"
end
```

There is nothing special about the name *run*. I just picked it to send the message to the object to get started. It returns a Boolean value of true or false depending on whether it worked. You could have made the run method just print out a final message, too.

5. Save the code before moving on to the next section. You can test it, too, and Ruby will remind you that the CodeBreaker class is missing. You'll write that next.

Creating Placeholder Classes

There are only two classes in this project. The main CodeBreaker class does the work of managing the program, dealing with the user's files that will be encoded or decoded, and displaying the user interface. The Caesar class implements the encryption code. By breaking the encoding functionality out this way, you can easily swap in other forms of encryption.

The CodeBreaker class

You'll use some familiar techniques for the main worker class:

1. Just below the top of the file's comments, define the class body and initialization method:

```
class CodeBreaker
  def initialize
    @input_file   = ''
    @output_file  = ''
    @password     = ''
  end
# Put the rest of the code here
end
```

Here you're clearing out some instance variables with empty strings. You'll use that to mean no filename has been selected by the user yet or no password is being used.

Recall that in Ruby only two values are recognized to be false: the keyword `nil` and `false`. Everything else is considered to be true with respect to how conditions work. In this project, you're using the empty string to mean no filename for `@input_file` and `@output_file`. If you were to test those variables by themselves to see if they were true or false in a condition, they would be considered true. Be careful as you learn other languages — many languages treat empty strings as false when used in conditions.

2. Add a temporary run method inside of the `CodeBreaker` class:

```
def run
    true
end
```

This is the only method that the main program calls, so you'll skip stubbing out the rest of the implementation until the next section.

3. Save and run your program. The current `CodeBreaker` class doesn't do much other than act as a placeholder, but you'll be able to test and run the project now and shouldn't get an error. You can change the `true` to `false` to see the other message.

The Caesar class

Interestingly, the encryption class wasn't even used in the main class in the last section. Go ahead and create a placeholder anyway:

1. Above the `CodeBreaker` class, enter the `Caesar` class:

    ```
    class Caesar
    # Code will go here
    end
    ```

2. Save the file and test again. Yes, it is a bit anticlimactic, but things get interesting in the next section.

Coding CodeBreaker Methods

In the Code Breaker project, I show you the code in a top-down manner. The main class is responsible for all the input and output of the program. The class gathers the user's preferences and data, and then writes out a new file that contains the encrypted results.

You also create the ability to run the process in reverse and take an encoded file and translate it back into something that is hopefully readable.

The CodeBreaker run method

The main project code creates an instance of the `CodeBreaker` class and sends it one message, `run`, to get started. The `run` method is the only entry point of the entire object.

An *entry point* is simply the starting place for some specific functionality of a program. Programmers also talk about *application programming interfaces* (APIs). An API is the part of a class or program that other programmers see and use to access the provided functionality.

Implement the entry point inside of the `CodeBreaker` class by replacing the `run` stub:

```
def run
  if get_command && get_input_file && get_output_
    file && get_secret
    process_files
    true
  else
    false
  end
end
```

The `run` method is calling a series of other methods in the `if` statement. The `&&` symbol means "and." Each of the methods will return `true` if it is successful or `false` if it is not. In order to continue running, all the methods must be true.

The lines with the `true` value inside the `if` statement and the `false` line by itself after the `else` statement are going to be the return values for this method. Remember that you use those values to decide which text to print out as a final message in the main program.

User interface methods

The user interface for Code Breaker is going to ask the user what operation she wants to do (encrypt or decrypt the input file). The program will also request the name of the input file to use and the name of the file to write the results out to.

1. Create a constant array object that will contain the values you'll use to represent commands:

   ```
   COMMANDS = ['e', 'd']
   ```

   Put this line at the top of the `CodeBreaker` class just before the initialize method.

I'm using the letter *e* for the encrypt option and the letter *d* for decrypt. You can spell out the words, if you like.

This is a short array, but you could also write the array this way: COMMANDS = %w(e d). That looks a little funny but means the same thing.

2. Write the method that will display the menu of commands and collect the user's choice of operation:

```
def get_command
  print "Do you want to (e)ncrypt or (d)ecrypt a
    file? "
  @command = gets.chomp.downcase
  if !COMMANDS.include?(@command)
    puts "Unknown command, sorry!"
    return false
  end
  true
end
```

Here you get to use a few shortcuts of techniques you saw in previous projects. Ruby objects let you connect a series of method calls together. This is convenient, although it can be fragile if done too much. The line @command = gets.chomp. downcase reads in the user's command, removes the tailing newline character, and makes sure the letter is lowercase. This makes it easier for you to check if they made a valid choice.

In Step 1, you defined the valid commands in the COMMANDS array constant variable. Because it's an array, you can use any array method you might find useful when accessing the variable. !COMMANDS.include?(@command) uses the include? method to see if the value in the instance variable is inside of the array. This saves a bunch of typing. You could've written the check using multiple if conditions. The exclamation point means "not," so the whole condition would read "if the command is not in the valid list of commands" (if you were to convert it to English).

3. Gather the user's choice of an input file next:

```
def get_input_file
  print "Enter the name of the input file: "
  @input_file = gets.chomp
  # Check to see if the files exist
  if !File.exists?(@input_file)
    puts "Can't find the input file, sorry!"
    return false
  end
  true
end
```

This one should look mostly familiar based on what you've learned up until now. The new code in the condition checks to see if a file exists in your project directory with the name that was entered by the user. This file must exist for the program to work because it's the input for the algorithm.

The `File` class provides all kinds of useful functionality for reading and writing files, as well as for doing other things with files that are familiar to you if you use your computer's file management tools like Explorer or Finder.

4. Create a nearly identical method to the last input file method to get an output filename from the user:

```
def get_output_file
  print "Enter the name of the output file: "
  @output_file = gets.chomp
  if File.exists?(@output_file)
    puts "The output file already exists, can't
    overwrite"
    return false
  end
  true
end
```

Can you spot the subtle difference between the input and output file methods' `if` statements? Both are checking for existence, but what else is different?

The output file will be used by the program to save the results of the encryption algorithm. Here you want to be sure that the file does *not* exist; otherwise, you'd destroy it with the new output. The `!` (not) symbol is absent in this condition, which is really important, because you want to know when the file actually does exist.

5. Lastly, collect the user's choice of a password:

```
def get_secret
  print "Enter the secret password: "
  @password = gets.chomp
end
```

There are no special conditional checks on this method. Whatever the user enters for a secret is fine. You'll see why in a bit.

You might be wondering why you don't have to return a `true` or `false` here. Remember that Ruby returns the results of the last statement of a method as the return value for the method. The last line here assigns the input from `gets.chomp` to the instance variable `@password`, and that will be the result. Recall that any value other than `nil` or `false` is considered true. For the condition in the `run` method to pass, the user can enter anything at all. If you cared about what the return result was specifically (as you did in the other methods), you could instead return `true` or `false` explicitly. You don't have to worry too much about this in this program.

6. Save your code and try running it. You should get some prompts, but what do you answer for the input file (see Figure 8-2)?

```
●  ●  ●                    project08 — bash — 80×24
Christophers-MacBook-Pro:project08 chaupt$ ruby codebreak.rb
Code Breaker will encrypt or decrypt a file of your choice

Do you want to (e)ncrypt or (d)ecrypt a file? e
Enter the name of the input file: message.txt
Can't find the input file, sorry!
Didn't work!
Christophers-MacBook-Pro:project08 chaupt$ █
```

Figure 8-2: You need an external input file to encode.

7. Using Atom, create a new file and call it message.txt. The name is not important, so if you want to call it something else, that's fine — just use that name for input in later steps. You may enter any content you like:

```
Friends, Romans, countrymen, lend me your ears;
I come to bury Caesar, not to praise him.
The evil that men do lives after them;
The good is oft interred with their bones;
So let it be with Caesar. The noble Brutus
Hath told you Caesar was ambitious:
If it were so, it was a grievous fault,
And grievously hath Caesar answer'd it.
Here, under leave of Brutus and the rest--
For Brutus is an honourable man;
So are they all, all honourable men--


Antony
```

8. Save the message file in the project08 directory next to your codebreak.rb file and run the program again, using the filename you choose for the input file prompt. You will get further (see Figure 8-3), but it's time to implement the file processing code.

```
● ● ●                    🗎 project08 — bash — 80×24
Christophers-MacBook-Pro:project08 chaupt$ ruby codebreak.rb
Code Breaker will encrypt or decrypt a file of your choice

Do you want to (e)ncrypt or (d)ecrypt a file? e
Enter the name of the input file: message.txt
Enter the name of the output file: secret.txt
Enter the secret password: Brutus
codebreak.rb:58:in `run': undefined local variable or method `process_files' for
 #<CodeBreaker:0x007fbba3188f38> (NameError)
        from codebreak.rb:69:in `<main>'
Christophers-MacBook-Pro:project08 chaupt$ ▊
```

Figure 8-3: The user interface appears to be working, but the processing is missing.

Encryption and decryption methods

The main work of Code Breaker is done when it processes your input file and creates an output file with the results.

1. The file processing method will be inside the `CodeBreaker` class. I'll show it to you in pieces. Start with the method definition:

   ```
   def process_files
   ```

2. Instantiate an encoder object using the `Caesar` class:

   ```
   encoder = Caesar.new(@password.size)
   ```

I'm using the words *encoder* and *encryption* as well as *decoder* and *decryption* somewhat interchangeably for this program.

The Caesar cipher doesn't really use a password or secret key, but other algorithms do. The `CodeBreaker` class is set up so you could swap out the `Caesar` class with another class that needs a real password. Because the Caesar cipher just needs a number for how many positions to shift the alphabet, you just use the length of the word(s) that the user enters at the prompt. That means that you can get the same results with two words that are the same size. Yes, `dogs` and `cats` would be the same thing — shocking!

3. Ruby's `File` class is actually a special version of another class called `IO` (short for input output). First, open up an output file to hold the results of the algorithm:

```
File.open(@output_file, "w") do |output|
```

Here you're telling Ruby to open the file that is held by the `@output_file` instance variable and that you'll be writing to it (the `w`). The local variable `output` will be how you access the file.

4. Next, you want to open up the input file and read each line of the file. Ruby's `IO` class gives you a nice tool for doing just that:

```
IO.foreach(@input_file) do |line|
```

All in one shot, Ruby can open the file named by the value in `@input_file`, and it will read each line and place that data in the local `line` variable.

5. Take the input line and convert it based on the user's choice of operations. Remember that the user picked to either encrypt or decrypt the file, so this needs to work in either direction:

```
converted_line = convert(encoder, line)
```

Here you use a method that I haven't shown you yet called `convert`. It takes as arguments the `encoder` object and the current input `line`. It returns the data in either an encrypted or decrypted form.

6. We want to write out the line to store it in another file. You could actually write this all out to the screen, but I think a file is better for now:

```
output.puts converted_line
```

The `puts` is familiar to you, isn't it? When you use `puts` all by itself, it just writes output to the screen. If you send the `puts` message to a file, such as the one that is stored in the local variable `output`, it will write the contents of the `converted_line` variable there instead.

When `puts` writes its output to the screen, programmers call that destination *standard output* (or *standard out* for short, and *stdout* for an even shorter abbreviation). As you might have guessed, *gets* can work in much the same way, and when you use it as you do in this program, you're reading from *standard input* (or *standard in* or *stdin*).

7. Finish the method with all the missing `end` statements:

```
        end
      end
    end
```

I broke the method up quite a bit, so here is the whole thing and what it should look like:

```
def process_files
  encoder = Caesar.new(@password.size)
  File.open(@output_file, "w") do |output|
    IO.foreach(@input_file) do |line|
      converted_line = convert(encoder, line)
      output.puts converted_line
    end
  end
end
```

8. Add the missing `convert` method:

```
def convert(encoder, string)
  if @command == 'e'
    encoder.encrypt(string)
  else
    encoder.decrypt(string)
  end
end
```

This method simply switches which method will be used on the encoder object based on the user's choice of commands. The return value of the encoder object will be the return value of this method, too.

9. Save your work. If you test it now, you'll get an error like in Figure 8-4, complaining that your `Caesar` class's `initialize` method has the wrong number of arguments. Time to fix that.

```
● ● ●                      project08 — bash — 80×24
Christophers-MacBook-Pro:project08 chaupt$ ruby codebreak.rb
Code Breaker will encrypt or decrypt a file of your choice

Do you want to (e)ncrypt or (d)ecrypt a file? e
Enter the name of the input file: message.txt
Enter the name of the output file: output.txt
Enter the secret password: brutus
codebreak.rb:64:in `initialize': wrong number of arguments (1 for 0) (ArgumentEr
ror)
        from codebreak.rb:64:in `new'
        from codebreak.rb:64:in `process_files'
        from codebreak.rb:75:in `run'
        from codebreak.rb:86:in `<main>'
Christophers-MacBook-Pro:project08 chaupt$ 
```

Figure 8-4: Getting closer, but your Caesar class isn't quite set up correctly yet.

Coding Caesar Methods

The Caesar cipher algorithm will be implemented within the Caesar class. By creating a class that has a standard set of methods, it's possible to swap out the Caesar class for another one that implements the same methods but uses a different algorithm.

Programmers like to create common interfaces, or APIs, to allow flexibility in their programs. It allows you to easily upgrade and experiment with other approaches in the future.

Setup methods

In the "Seeing how the Caesar cipher works" section, earlier in this chapter, you take two copies of the alphabet, line them up next to each other, and shift the encrypted one by some number of positions. If you position the two copies of the alphabet side by side, as in Figure 8-1, you can use them as a kind of table to look up each letter. Depending on whether you're encrypting or decrypting a message, you start with the plain or shifted alphabet, respectively.

1. Create the updated `Caesar` class initialize method to set up the copies of the alphabet you'll need:

```
def initialize(shift)
  alphabet_lower = 'abcdefghijklmnopqrstuvwxyz'
```

You start with the plain alphabet.

2. The Caesar cipher isn't really smart about uppercase versus lowercase characters. In the project's lookup table, it's very literal, so you need to include the uppercase letters explicitly:

```
alphabet_upper = alphabet_lower.upcase
alphabet = alphabet_lower + alphabet_upper
```

Using your knowledge of string methods, you can automatically convert the lowercase alphabet to an uppercase one, and then add the two together so your copy of the alphabet contains both cases.

3. For the encrypted version of the alphabet, you need to shift it a certain number of positions. The `shift` parameter of the `initialize` method contains that number. But what happens if that number is too big? Let's use some math to make sure that the number used will always be less than the length of our array:

```
index = shift % alphabet.size
```

You need the length of the alphabet string, which should be two times the length of the standard English alphabet (2 × 26 = 52). You then use that value and divide the shift number using the modulo operator (%). Modulo division gives you the remainder of the division. Think back to doing long division in math class. If your shift number was 3 and alphabet length was 52, how many times does 52 go in to 3? Zero times. How many items are left over though? You end up with a remainder of three. Likewise, if your shift number was 53, then 53 divided by 52 is 1 with a remainder of 1. We never want our index variable to be bigger than the size of the alphabet minus 1. Try this out on paper or with IRB to prove to yourself that it works!

4. Build the encrypted version by grabbing parts of the alphabet and swapping them around using Ruby's string methods:

```
encrypted_alphabet = alphabet[index..-1] +
    alphabet[0...index]
```

Be careful to get the punctuation marks correct here. There are two periods in the first part and three in the other.

The syntax is a little odd looking, but let me break it down. By using the square brackets on a string, you can work with the string in a manner that is similar to an array. You can provide an index number into the string, and you'll get the appropriate character (letter) for that position. If you provide a range of indexes, you get that fraction of the string that encompasses the starting and ending letters described in the range. Programmers call this a *substring*. In this code, you're building a new string by taking the later part of the alphabet starting at the number inside of index and going to the end (alphabet[index..-1]), and then adding on the front part of the alphabet starting at the first letter up to and including the letter at the position of index (alphabet[0...index]).

5. Wrap up the `initialize` method by calling out to another method for further setup:

```
setup_lookup_tables(alphabet,
    encrypted_alphabet)
end
```

It isn't completely necessary to break this setup into a separate method, but I'm doing it to introduce the Ruby hash class.

6. Define the lookup table method and initialize some instance variables:

```
def setup_lookup_tables(decrypted_alphabet,
    encrypted_alphabet)
  @encryption_hash = {}
  @decryption_hash = {}
```

The `decrypted_alphabet` parameter holds the regular alphabet. The new syntax of {} means an empty hash, and is similar to the array syntax you used in other projects. You'll fill in the hashes next.

7. The plan here is to loop through the length of the alphabet and, for each letter, fill in one of two lookup tables. One table will be used to go from unencoded text to encoded text (encryption), and the other will go from encoded text to decoded text (decryption).

```
0.upto(decrypted_alphabet.size) do |index|
  @encryption_hash[decrypted_alphabet[index]] =
  encrypted_alphabet[index]
  @decryption_hash[encrypted_alphabet[index]] =
  decrypted_alphabet[index]
  end
end
```

You've used the `upto` looping method before, and it's going to loop the same number of times as the size of your alphabet. The two lines inside the block load up the hashes. The index number from the loop is used as an index for the string, and it works much like an index in an array to return a specific position's letter.

The syntax for accessing a hash is similar to an array in that it uses square brackets, but rather than a number as an index, the index can be anything. You're using the letters from your alphabets in this project. On the right side of the equal (assignment) sign, you use the index number to read into the other alphabet string to get that position's letter. You could draw this out like a table if you wanted to see how the letters map back and forth.

A hash primer

Hashes, sometimes called hash maps or dictionaries, are another core Ruby data structure. I consider hashes (along with arrays) to be one of the most useful objects when implementing programs.

Hashes are a container data structure, and like arrays, they have individual locations that can hold any kind of object. Instead of slots that are indexed numerically, content in hashes are indexed via a key, which can be almost any kind of object. Typically, the key is a string or Ruby symbol. In the project in this chapter, you're using an alphabetic letter or number, but always in the form of a string.

You can think of hashes like an English dictionary or the index pages at the back of a book work. You can look up a word by name, and it will return a definition or page number, respectively.

Hashes are not a fixed size — they grow (or shrink) as needed. Once a hash is created with a blank hash via either { } or `Hash.new`, you can start adding objects to a hash by providing a key. For instance, if `my_hash = { }` were set up, I could store a string that holds a nearby city using my name as a key with the code `my_hash['chris'] = 'San Francisco'`.

To retrieve a value, you simply use the same key `my_hash['chris']`, and Ruby will return whatever is stored there.

If you use a key that doesn't exist, by default Ruby will return `nil`.

In the Caesar cipher code, you're using a hash as a lookup table. This means that if you know one of the letters of the string you're processing, and you know which hash to use, you can use that letter as the key, and the hash will return the stored encrypted letter that corresponds to that letter as the value. For example, `@encryption_hash['a']` contains the letter `x` if the shift amount was 3.

Encryption and decryption methods

Most of the hard work in this class was setting up hashes for the lookup tables. Now you'll create the encryption and decryption functions that use them:

1. Write the code for encrypting a string first:

```
def encrypt(string)
  result = []
  string.each_char do |c|
    if @encryption_hash[c]
      result << @encryption_hash[c]
    else
      result << c
    end
  end
  result.join
end
```

The method starts by setting up an empty array to hold the translated letters. The `each_char` method of the Ruby string class will loop through the given string stored inside the `string` local variables. It returns each character in turn. For each character, it uses the value as the key for the

@encryption_hash hash. If the key is valid, Ruby returns the character — first in the condition to see if it exists, and then again to append it to the results array. If the key is not in the @encryption_hash, it returns nil, which Ruby treats like false. In that case, the else clause is used and the character is appended to the results as is. Finally, the array join method is called on the return value. The join method takes each item in the array and smashes it together to make a string.

2. The decryption method is almost exactly the same. The only difference is which hash is used:

```ruby
def decrypt(string)
  result = []
  string.each_char do |c|
    if @decryption_hash[c]
      result << @decryption_hash[c]
    else
      result << c
    end
  end
  result.join
end
```

3. Save your code and try running the program now. It should run and look something like Figure 8-5.

```
● ● ●                    project08 — bash — 80×24
Christophers-MacBook-Pro:project08 chaupt$ ruby codebreak.rb
Code Breaker will encrypt or decrypt a file of your choice

Do you want to (e)ncrypt or (d)ecrypt a file? e
Enter the name of the input file: message.txt
Enter the name of the output file: secret.txt
Enter the secret password: brutus
All done!
Christophers-MacBook-Pro:project08 chaupt$ 
```

Figure 8-5: Now you can encrypt (or decrypt) a message file.

In my example, I saved my encrypted `message.txt` contents out to the file `secret.txt` file. It looks like this after encryption:

```
Lxoktjy, Xusgty, iuAtzxEskt, rktj sk EuAx kgxy;
O iusk zu hAxE Igkygx, tuz zu vxgoyk nos.
Znk kBor zngz skt ju roBky glzkx znks;
Znk muuj oy ulz otzkxxkj Cozn znkox hutky;
Yu rkz oz hk Cozn Igkygx. Znk tuhrk HxAzAy
Ngzn zurj EuA Igkygx Cgy gshozouAy:
Ol oz Ckxk yu, oz Cgy g mxokBuAy lgArz,
Gtj mxokBuAyrE ngzn Igkygx gtyCkx'j oz.
Nkxk, Atjkx rkgBk ul HxAzAy gtj znk xkyz--
Lux HxAzAy oy gt nutuAxghrk sgt;
Yu gxk znkE grr, grr nutuAxghrk skt--

GtzutE
```

So indeed! It is a little harder to read isn't it? If I send my `secret.txt` file back through the program again with the same secret password, I should get back my original text like in Figure 8-6.

```
● ● ●                    project08 — bash — 80×24
Christophers-MacBook-Pro:project08 chaupt$ ruby codebreak.rb
Code Breaker will encrypt or decrypt a file of your choice

Do you want to (e)ncrypt or (d)ecrypt a file? d
Enter the name of the input file: secret.txt
Enter the name of the output file: final.txt
Enter the secret password: brutus
All done!
Christophers-MacBook-Pro:project08 chaupt$ cat final.txt
Friends, Romans, countrymen, lend me your ears;
I come to bury Caesar, not to praise him.
The evil that men do lives after them;
The good is oft interred with their bones;
So let it be with Caesar. The noble Brutus
Hath told you Caesar was ambitious:
If it were so, it was a grievous fault,
And grievously hath Caesar answer'd it.
Here, under leave of Brutus and the rest--
For Brutus is an honourable man;
So are they all, all honourable men--

Antony
Christophers-MacBook-Pro:project08 chaupt$ █
```

Figure 8-6: The decrypted message file.

Trying Some Experiments

You can experiment with lots of things in this project. The Caesar cipher itself is relatively simple (and easy to figure out by experienced code breakers). With the way the code is structured, it should be easy to swap out the `Caesar` class with another one that uses the same basic API.

You also learned a fair bit about using hashes and a little regarding file input and output. These techniques will be useful as you build more sophisticated programs.

- In the Caesar class, I spelled out the alphabet by manually typing out each letter. Try substituting this Ruby instead and see what it does: `('a'..'z').to_a.join`.

- If you enter a message that has numbers in it, what happens? How might you fix this problem?

- I showed you how to capture the output of the encoder into a file. What if you wanted to see it show up onscreen instead?

- The Ruby string class has a method called `tr`, which can transform one string to another. Look it up in the Ruby documentation and see if you can replace the body of the Caesar `encrypt` and `decrypt` methods using the `tr` method instead. *Hint:* You can do the whole thing in one line!

Acey Deucey

As you become more comfortable with thinking like an object-oriented programmer, it becomes second nature to break projects down into objects that represent real-world concepts. You can imagine what the objects look like and how they behave. When you combine your ability to program objects with a rich library of built-in features like Ruby's, you'll find that you can create some pretty sophisticated projects without as much work as you might have to do in another programming language.

In this project, you're going to combine a set of custom objects together with heavy use of Ruby's array class to build a multi-player card game called Acey Deucey, which requires you to create a number of objects, such as playing cards, a deck, players, and the game rules.

```
● ● ●                    project09 — ruby — 80×24
Christophers-MacBook-Pro:project09 chaupt$ ruby acey.rb
Welcome to Acey Deucy
Enter number of players: 3
Enter name for player #1: Amy
Enter name for player #2: Bert
Enter name for player #3: Chris
Amy has 10 chips
Bert has 10 chips
Chris has 10 chips
-------------------------------------------
Round 1! The dealer has 0 chips.
-------------------------------------------
Everyone antes
The dealer now has 3 chips.
---> Current cards:
Player Amy
7 of Clubs
10 of Hearts

Player Bert
Jack of Spades
Jack of Hearts

Player Chris
```

Organizing a New Project

This projects requires that you use Atom to create and edit your program. This time, you'll store the project's source code in multiple Ruby files, one for each object's class. You'll continue to use the Terminal program to run, test, and play the game.

If you haven't created a development folder already, refer to Project 2 for instructions on how to do that.

1. Start your Terminal program and enter the development folder:

   ```
   $ cd development
   ```

2. Create a new directory for this project:

   ```
   $ mkdir project09
   ```

3. Move in to the new directory:

   ```
   $ cd project09
   ```

4. Start Atom by double-clicking its icon.

5. Create a new source code file by choosing File ⇨ New File. Save it by choosing File ⇨ Save and store it in your project09 directory. Call the file acey.rb. As you work through the project, you'll create all your other files in the same directory.

If some of these steps are confusing to you, refer to the "Organizing a New Project" section from Project 4. It provides more details for each step.

Planning the Project

The game of Acey Deucey has been around for many years and has many local variations of its rules. The basic idea, though, is that you have one deck of standard playing cards for two or more players in the game. The players will play rounds of the game until either the deck runs out or all the players have been eliminated except one. Whichever player has the most chips at the end is declared the winner.

This game is pretty simple, but you still need to get your plan together to make it easy to write the program.

The main object starts up the game engine and determines how many and who the players are. The main object will have just enough code to launch the game, but it won't contain any actual game rules.

Perhaps the most important object in the project is the one that represents the game itself. This object manages rounds of the game, acts as the "dealer" passing out cards, and requests that the players make bets on whether cards will be a winning or losing hand. All the rules for the game will be here.

A third object will represent the players of the game. The player object will store information about the player like her name, her number of virtual chips or coins used to place bets, and the actual cards in her hand.

Finally, you need a deck of playing cards. In this project, you break down the problem into two different classes of objects. There will be individual playing cards, each storing its rank (its face value, like 2, 10, Jack, Ace, or Queen) and its suit (diamonds, hearts, clubs, or spades). The card objects will be stored together in another object that represents the deck. The deck class knows how to hold, shuffle, and deal cards, but doesn't care what the cards themselves are like.

Splitting up the code into a number of classes of objects lets you think about parts of the game at higher (or lower) levels. I'll show you the details in a mostly bottom-up manner in this project.

The rules of Acey Deucey

The card game Acey Deucey has been around a long time. As a relatively simple game, it allows you to explore object-oriented programming at the same time as you learn to program some slightly more involved game rules or logic. There are many variations of the game, so let me describe the rules you'll use for this project.

The dealer starts with a standard deck of 52 playing cards (where the 2 card is low and the Ace card is high). The suits (Diamonds, Hearts, and so on) don't matter in this variation. The dealer shuffles the cards to prepare for a game.

Each player has a stack of chips used to make bets. At the start of a round of play, each player *antes* (contributes) one or more chips to the dealer's bank (sometimes calls a *pot*).

Next, the dealer deals two cards to each player. In the real world, these cards are face up, so everyone can see them. The dealer goes around the table for each player and asks the player to bet on whether a third card will be in between the player's two cards, as measured by the rank of the card. If a player has a 3 of Hearts and a 10 of Spades, the player needs to guess whether her next card will be a 4, 5, 6, 7, 8, or 9 of any suit. She can bet any number of chips between 0 and either the number of chips she has or the total number of chips in the dealer's bank, whichever is smaller.

The dealer then flips over a third card. If that card is between the first two cards, the player wins and collects the number of chips she bet from the bank.

If the flipped over card is outside of the two cards (so either a 2 or a Jack, Queen, King, or Ace), she loses her bet and must pay that to the dealer's bank.

If the flipped card is exactly the same rank as either of the first two cards (another 3 or 10), then the player loses *double* her bet — ouch!

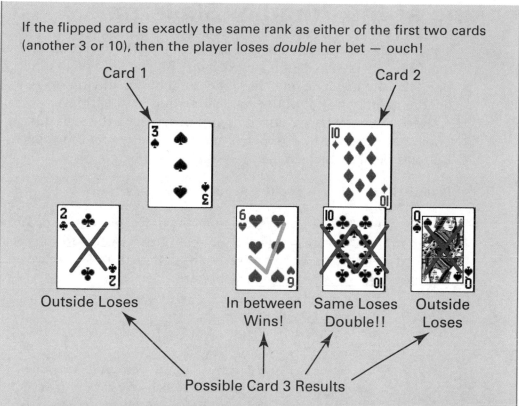

Card 1

Card 2

Outside Loses

In between Wins!

Same Loses Double!!

Outside Loses

Possible Card 3 Results

Play continues around the table until everyone has had a turn. That ends the first round, and play continues for another round as long as there are enough cards to continue.

In this version, if the bank runs out of chips, the dealer will require that all players ante up again. If a player runs out of chips, she is eliminated from the game.

The game ends when either the deck no longer has enough cards for a round or all players but one are eliminated. The player with the most chips at the end is the winner.

Looking at the Program Skeleton

The code in this project uses a handful of classes to represent the main objects involved with a card game. As you've seen in other projects, there will be one piece of code that has the job of creating the main object(s) of the application and getting things started. You may have noticed as you progressed through this book that the code that launches and runs the rest of the application has been getting simpler and simpler as you go.

Follow these steps to create the main program's code:

1. For Acey Deucey, the `acey.rb` file is your game's main program file. It creates and uses the rest of the objects to run the card game. Start with your standard comment to let the world know what this program is all about:

   ```
   #
   # Ruby For Kids Project 9: Acey Deucy
   # Programmed By: Chris Haupt
   # A multiplayer card game where you try to guess
       whether the next card will be between two
       other cards, placing bets on the results
   #
   ```

2. In this project, you use separate source code files to store each of the classes you create. Programmers use this technique to keep file size smaller and more manageable. Once a file gets to be much more than a full screen's worth of code, it gets harder to read and maintain. Ruby doesn't care whether the code is in one file or many, but if you do use more than one file, you need to give Ruby a clue where to find those other files. Do that next:

   ```
   require_relative "game"
   require_relative "deck"
   require_relative "card"
   require_relative "player"
   ```

require_relative tells Ruby that the file that starts with the supplied name is in the same directory as the current code. You can put code anywhere, and give Ruby the path to the code, but keep things simple for now and use the same folder.

3. The Acey Deucey game has a couple of constant variables that can be used to tune the game, so add those next:

```
STARTING_NUMBER_OF_CHIPS = 10
MINIMUM_PLAYERS          = 2
```

4. The purpose of the acey.rb file is to create the starting objects and launch the game. First up is setting up player objects. Ask the user of the program how many players she wants to simulate:

```
puts "Welcome to Acey Deucy"
print "Enter number of players: "
player_count = gets
player_count = player_count.to_i
```

gets returns a string, so you're using the to_i method to transform the string into a number. Ruby ignores whitespace when it does the conversion, so you don't need to chomp off the newline character as you've done in the past.

5. Confirm that the minimum number of players has been requested and prepare an array to hold the player objects. You'll add the rest of that code in a moment. Also, add a message in the else condition to let the user know that she needs to pick another number of players:

```
if player_count >= MINIMUM_PLAYERS
  # Load up some players
  players = []
 # Add code to create players here
else
  puts "There should be at least
    #{MINIMUM_PLAYERS}"
end
```

6. Now go back in the body of the `if` condition and create some player objects. Add this code in place of the `Add code to create players here` comment:

```
(0...player_count).each do |index|
  print "Enter name for player ##{index + 1}: "
  name = gets
  name = name.chomp
  players << Player.new(name, STARTING_NUMBER_
    OF_CHIPS)
end
```

You should recognize most of the methods here. You're looping the number of times needed to create `player_count` objects. For each player object, you gather string input for the player's name. Then you create the actual `Player` object, passing in the name and some amount of chips to be used by that player.

7. You have everything you need to create the main `Game` object that will take over and run the game. Add this code right after the player creation loop:

```
game_engine = Game.new(players)
game_engine.show_player_chips
game_engine.play
```

You take three steps to launch the game. First you create the `Game` object from the `Game` class. You pass the players array to the game, and the `Game` object will manage the players for the rest of the program. Second, you use a method on the `Game` object to display the starting set of players. This is part of the program's user interface. Finally, the last line launches the game.

Creating Classes

The Acey Deucey program will use four classes to run the game. In this project, I show you these items from the bottom up, starting with the lower-level classes and then moving to the higher-level classes that use them. You should compare this technique with the top-down approach you've used in other projects. Which one makes more sense to you?

Creating the card class

Acey Deucy is a card game, so of course you'll need some object that represents the concept of a playing card. The card object will know what its suit and rank are, and how to compare itself with other cards to figure out which cards are "higher" or "lower" for the game. Because you're working bottom-up in your coding, you need to think a bit about the functionality required by higher-level classes.

1. Switch over to Atom and create a new file called `card.rb`. Make sure that you save this file in the same directory as the `acey.rb` main program. Create the class definition:

   ```
   class Card
   # Code goes here
   end
   ```

2. This game uses standard playing cards. Create two arrays that hold the suits and ranks of cards and place them inside of the class:

   ```
   SUITS = %w(Clubs Diamonds Hearts Spades)
   RANKS = %w(2 3 4 5 6 7 8 9 10 Jack Queen
       King Ace)
   ```

Here you're using the shorthand `%w()` syntax for Ruby arrays that contain a list of strings. You could've written this as `SUITS = ["Clubs", "Diamonds", "Hearts", "Spades"]`, but since the items in each array are single words (or numbers treated as words), the shorthand works to save a bit of typing.

3. The outside world needs to be able to get the card's suit and rank, so use Ruby's `accessor` functions:

   ```
   attr_accessor :rank, :suit
   ```

   Accessors can also be used in the class, and you'll notice that when you want to use the variable's value elsewhere in the program, you're using the accessor instead of the instance variable name (the one with the @ sign). For your purposes, this is a programmer preference thing.

4. When the card is created, its suit and rank will be assigned to it, so create an `initialize` method to accept those values:

   ```
   def initialize(rank, suit)
     @rank = rank
     @suit = suit
   end
   ```

5. In the user interface of the game, you'll want to print out what the card is, so use Ruby convention for the name of a method to print out an object as a string:

   ```
   def to_s
     "#{rank} of #{suit}"
   end
   ```

   Here you're using the accessors for the two variables. You could've used `@rank` and `@suit`. Your choice.

Almost all objects in Ruby have a `to_s` method (which means "to string"). Sometimes the built in `to_s` isn't as useful as you'd like, so you can override the default behavior by defining your own method as you're doing here. For the `Card` class, you're just returning a string you make by combining the rank and suit using string interpolation.

6. Ruby has a built-in method for comparing two values and determining if the first is less than, equal to, or greater than the second one. Create a comparison method that you'll use later on to create the game's rules:

```
# returns  -1 if card1 is less than, 0 if same
    as, and 1 if larger than card2
def self.compare_rank(card1, card2)
  RANKS.index(card1.rank) <=> RANKS.index(card2.
  rank)
end
```

There are a couple of things going on here that are new:

- The word `self` in the method definition tells Ruby that this method is a *class method*. A class method is a message you send to the class itself rather than an instance of (an object made from) the class. This is super helpful when you need to create some code that relates to a class but needs to work outside of specific objects.

- The `<=>` symbol (which Ruby calls the *spaceship operator*) is used by Ruby to compare the two objects on the left and right of the symbol. For this program, you're using the `Array` class's `index` method to find the position in the `RANKS` array of the two cards' ranks. When you have those numbers, you compare the positions to see if the first card is less than, equal to, or greater than the second card.

7. You need a way to create a collection of all 52 playing cards that can be used as a deck. Create a *factory method* on the class that will do this work:

```
def self.create_cards
  cards = []
  SUITS.each do |suit|
    RANKS.each do |rank|
      cards << Card.new(rank, suit)
    end
  end
  cards
end
```

This is another class method and can be called to make a new deck of cards. It has two loops: The outside one loops through the SUITS array, and for each suit, an inner loop goes through the RANKS array to create each card. The method returns the array of all cards, just like a brand-new deck!

Programmers call functions that create objects *factory methods*. I suppose that's because a factory is a place that makes things!

8. Save your code before moving on.

Creating the deck class

The card class creates a deck of cards, but doesn't really know anything about the behavior of a deck of cards. The deck class will have that job.

1. Create a new file called deck.rb in the same directory as the other files. Add the class's definition:

```
class Deck
# Code goes here
end
```

2. Create the initialization method that takes an array of cards as its argument:

```
def initialize(cards)
  @cards = cards
end
```

3. One thing decks of cards can do is have their cards be randomly shuffled, so add that method:

```
def shuffle
  unless @cards.empty?
    @cards.shuffle!
  end
end
```

The `unless` keyword in Ruby is the opposite of the `if` condition keyword. It's exactly the same as saying "if not." I'm demonstrating it in this code for you, because sometimes it reads more clearly. If it's harder to understand, just switch the line to `if not @cards.empty?`, and you'll have the same meaning.

Because `@cards` holds an array object, you can use all of Ruby's built-in methods to implement your project. Here you're using the array method `empty?` to see if any cards remain in the array; if they do, the `shuffle!` method randomly mixes up the array. Ruby uses the convention of adding a question mark (`?`) at the end of a method if it generally returns a Boolean value, and an exclamation point (`!`) if the method somehow changes the associated object.

4. Decks of cards are also used to pass cards out to players (dealing), so create a method to do that:

```
def deal
  unless @cards.empty?
    @cards.pop
  end
end
```

5. In some card games, knowing how many cards are left in the deck is important, so add a method to get the deck's size:

```
def size
  @cards.length
end
```

6. Save your work.

Creating the player class

The player in Acey Deucy is going to have a name, some number of cards in her hand, a number of chips to place bets with, and a current bet number.

1. Create a `player.rb` file and add the class definition:

```
class Player
# Code goes here
end
```

2. The player has several attributes that you'll track and use, so create an accessor for them:

```
attr_accessor :name, :hand, :chips, :bet
```

3. Next, in the initializer for this class, you'll want to set up the starting values for everything:

```
def initialize(name, chips)
  @name = name
  @hand = []
  @chips = chips
  @bet  = nil
end
```

nil is Ruby's way of saying that the variable has no value at all. At the start of the game, you're representing the fact that the player doesn't have a current bet by using nil. Also, notice that the starting value for the player's hand of cards is an empty array []. You'll use an array to hold the player's cards (those Array objects are handy aren't they?).

4. The game needs some way to tell the user to discard her old hand of cards to get ready for the next round:

```
def discard_hand
    @bet = nil
    @hand = []
end
```

You use this method as a chance to reset the player's bet to nil, too, since each round will require a new bet.

5. The dealer is going to deal a card and the player needs to put it in her hand:

```
def take_card(card)
  @hand << card
end
```

6. To make the game implementation a little easier, give the player the ability to sort her cards from low to high, so the lowest-ranked card will always be first one, and the highest will be the second one:

```
def sort_hand_by_rank
    @hand.sort! do |card1, card2|
        Card.compare_rank(card1, card2)
    end
end
```

Ruby's `Array` class really is pretty cool. Here you're using the `sort!` method to arrange the hand array in order, and you're able to use your `Card` class's `compare_rank` method you created earlier. That's a lot of work with a little bit of code.

7. For this game, if the player doesn't have any chips, she is eliminated and can't play anymore. Create a method that the game can use to check this out:

```
def eliminated?
    @chips <= 0
end
```

In theory, the player can't have less than zero chips, but we're checking just in case we make a programming mistake someplace else.

8. You need to have some way for the player to pay up if she loses a bet:

```
def pay(amount)
    if amount > @chips
        pay = @chips
        @chips = 0
    else
        pay = amount
        @chips -= amount
    end
    pay
end
```

This code deals with two cases. In the first, you handle what happens if the amount owned by the player is larger than the number of chips she has. You're going to pay up whatever is left in the player's pile of chips, and then set the chip count to zero. If the player has enough chips left, you just subtract that amount from the player's total.

9. Finally, if the player wins a bet, you need to be able to send those winnings to the player to put in her pile of chips:

```
def win(amount)
    @chips += amount
end
```

10. Save your code!

Creating the Game class

So far so good. You've created all the individual kinds of objects that Acey Deucey needs to actually be played. Time to dive in to the game rules and user interface.

1. Create the game.rb file and define the class:

```
class Game
# Code goes here
end
```

2. Define the attributes you'll want to access, and define a useful constant:

```
attr_reader :players, :deck, :bank, :round
ANTE_AMOUNT = 1
```

The ante is how much each player needs to put in at the start of each round to help fund the dealer's bank.

3. The initialization method for this class sets up a number of instance variables that you'll mostly access through the accessors in Step 2:

```
def initialize(players)
    @players = players
    @deck = Deck.new(Card.create_cards)
    @deck.shuffle
    @bank = 0
    @round = 0
end
```

The `players` array is passed in to the `Game` object from the `acey.rb` main program. The `Game` object does the rest of the setup by using your `Card` and `Deck` classes to set up the playing cards.

4. Provide a method that the `Game` object can use to determine if there are any active players remaining. ***Remember:*** We're defining an active player in this game as one that still has chips to play with:

```
def remaining_players
    players.count {|player| !player.eliminated?}
end
```

This code uses the `Array` class's `count` method to loop through each item in the array. For each item, it calls the player object's `eliminated?` method. If it isn't true, it will increase the count by one. This one line is an example of how compact Ruby can be if you use all its built-in power.

5. Create the main game loop. This method looks super long, but it's *almost* all user interface code using `puts` to print out messages for you to see:

```
def play
    while deck.size > (players.length * 3) &&
    remaining_players > 1 do
        new_round
        puts "-" * 40
        puts "Round #{round}! The dealer has
#{bank} chips."
        puts "-" * 40
        puts "Everyone antes"
        ante
        puts "The dealer now has #{bank} chips."
        deal_cards(2)
        sort_cards
        puts "---> Current cards:\n"
        show_cards
        puts "---> Players bet:\n"
        players_bet
        puts "\n---> Dealer deals one more
card\n"
        deal_cards(1)
        show_cards
        puts "---> Determining results\n"
        determine_results
        puts "\n---> New standings\n"
        show_player_chips
        puts ""
    end
    game_over
end
```

If you ignore the output lines, you'll see that the remaining method calls represent the separate steps of the game's rules. You can almost read this out loud and get a feel for how the game is played.

The game uses a `while` loop to keep playing until either the deck is too small to do a complete round or there is only one player left.

6. At the start of each round, the game updates its counter and tells all the players to discard their hands:

```
def new_round
    @round += 1
    players.each do |player|
        player.discard_hand
    end
end
```

7. Next, each player needs to contribute a chip to the bank as part of the ante step:

```
def ante
    players.each do |player|
        if not player.eliminated?
            @bank = @bank + player.
pay(ANTE_AMOUNT)
        end
    end
end
```

I'm using the `not` keyword in the conditions in this code. You could also write that line as `if !player.eliminated?` to mean the same thing. Use the syntax that is easier for you to understand.

8. The dealer needs to give each player his or her cards next:

```
def deal_cards(num_of_cards)
    players.each do |player|
        next if player.eliminated?
        1.upto(num_of_cards) do
            player.take_card(deck.deal)
        end
    end
end
```

The `deal_cards` method is handy, because it can be used to deal any number of cards to the player. In Acey Deucey, you need to give each player cards twice: once for the initial two cards, and then again for the third card. This method can be used both times. Reuse is great!

You've probably noticed that many of the Game class's methods use the same pattern of code. They each loop through the `players` array and take some action by sending a message to the `player` (or other objects). In `deal_cards`, the one new keyword is the use of `next`. That line will skip to the next iteration of the loop if the trailing condition is true. You don't want to deal cards to eliminated players, so you bypass that work when the player is out of chips.

9. When the game has dealt the initial two cards to the players, you want them to sort their hands to make it easier to pick out the low and high cards later on:

```
def sort_cards
    players.each do |player|
        next if player.eliminated?
        player.sort_hand_by_rank
    end
end
```

10. Now it is time for the players to get involved. You want to ask
    each one to bet on his or her hand:

```ruby
def players_bet
    players.each do |player|
        if player.eliminated?
            puts "#{player.name} passes. (Out of
chips!)"
        else
            print "#{player.name} can bet between
0 and #{max_bet(player)}: "
            bet = gets.to_i
            if bet < 0 || bet > max_bet(player)
                bet = 0
            end
            puts "#{player.name} bet #{bet}"
            player.bet = bet
        end
    end
end
```

Players who are out of chips aren't playing the round, so you
skip them. For all other players, you need to ask them to bet
some chips. Each player's individual bet is either the total
number of chips in the bank or the number of chips the player
is holding, whichever is smaller. The logic in this method
checks those game rules. Notice how the player object then
holds the final bet amount as a kind of memory of this action.

11. Create the helper method used to determine the maximum bet
    allowed by the player:

```ruby
def max_bet(player)
    [player.chips, bank].min
end
```

This method uses a neat little method on the `Array` class. It will look inside the array and find the minimum (`min`) number in the array and return that. Because you want the lower amount of the player's chips in the banks, this is just the trick.

12. Create a user interface method to nicely display all the player's current chip amounts:

```
def show_player_chips
    players.each do |player|
        if player.eliminated?
            puts "#{player.name} has been
eliminated"
        else
            puts "#{player.name} has #{player.
chips} chips"
        end
    end
end
```

13. Create another user interface method to review the players' cards:

```
def show_cards
    players.each do |player|
        puts "Player #{player.name}"
        if player.eliminated?
            puts "Has been eliminated!"
        else
            player.hand.each do |card|
                puts card.to_s
            end
        end
        puts ""
    end
end
```

14. Maybe the most complicated method of the whole game is the one that runs the game's rules for determining if the player won or lost. I'll break it down a little bit:

```
def determine_results
    players.each do |player|
        if not player.eliminated?
            low_card = player.hand[0]
            high_card = player.hand[1]
            middle_card = player.hand[2]
```

For each player still in the game, get the player's cards. **Remember:** You sorted the first two into low and high cards. The last card in the hand array is the "third" card, which is the one that should be in the middle of the other two in order to win.

15. Write a set of three conditions to check each game rule. If the rule turns out to be true, calculate how many chips the player will pay or win.

```
if Card.compare_rank(low_card, middle_card) == 0
    || Card.compare_rank(high_card,middle_
    card) == 0
    puts "#{player.name} got an exact match, loses
    twice the bet!"
    chips = player.pay(player.bet * 2)
elsif Card.compare_rank(middle_card, low_card) < 0
    || Card.compare_rank(middle_card, high_card) > 0
    puts "#{player.name} wasn't inbetween loses
    the bet!"
    chips = player.pay(player.bet)
else
    puts "#{player.name} wins bet!"
    chips = -player.bet
    player.win(player.bet)
end
```

In each case, store the change in the number of chips so you can adjust the dealer's bank next. Note that in the winning case, you need to subtract the player's bet from the bank, which is why you store the negative number of chips in the `else` case.

16. Adjust the bank with the winnings or losses of the player. If the bank "runs out of chips," the rules require that all players ante up again until the bank has a positive number of chips:

```
        @bank = @bank + chips
        if @bank <= 0
                puts "Dealer is out of chips,
    everyone needs to ante up!"
        end
        while @bank <= 0
                ante
        end
            end
      end
  end
```

17. You're in the home stretch! Add a method to display the final messages at the end of the game:

```
def game_over
    puts "Game Over!"
    players.sort! do |player1, player2|
        player1.chips <=> player2.chips
    end
    puts "The winner is #{players.last.name}"
end
```

Here you're using the `Array` class's `sort!` method again and the spaceship operator to sort the players by their chip count, lowest to highest. The last player in the array is the one with the most chips.

18. Save your code and test your project. Fix any typos, particularly from the long lines in this class. The game should run, let you set up some players, and keep placing bets until the deck runs out or someone is the last player with chips (see Figure 9-1)!

```
● ● ●                    📄 project09 — bash — 80×24
Player Amy
Has been eliminated!

Player Bert
9 of Spades
10 of Clubs
King of Spades

Player Chris
7 of Diamonds
8 of Clubs
2 of Hearts

---> Determining results
Bert wasn't inbetween loses the bet!
Chris wasn't inbetween loses the bet!

---> New standings
Amy has been eliminated
Bert has 6 chips
Chris has 4 chips

Game Over!
The winner is Bert
```

Figure 9-1: Acey Deucy in action.

Trying Some Experiments

Now that you have objects that can be used for a card game, you can start to experiment with different rules to make up your own games.

Here are a few things to try to test your Ruby understanding:

- ✔ A number of the loops in the Game class used the next keyword. How would you write those loops without the next keyword?

- ✔ Change the rules of the game so that the players only ante once at the start of the game and again when the bank runs out of chips. How does that change the way the game is played?

✔ Check to see if the player has enough chips to play that round. She needs at least ANTE + 1 chips, why?

✔ This version of the game deals two cards to each player first, and then conducts the betting round. What would be different if you dealt only two cards to one player, had them bet, and then went on to the next player? Is that fair?

✔ How might you change the game to play multiple rounds, where you would start with a fresh deck of cards when the last deck ran out?

Part IV
Using Shared Code to Get Graphical

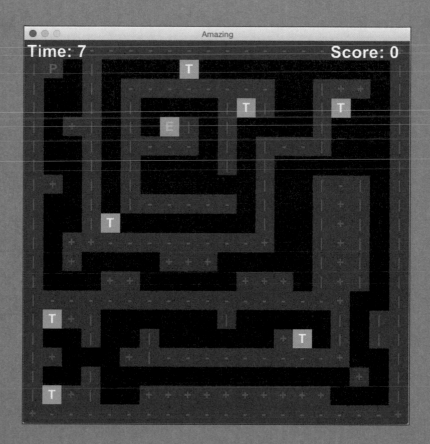

In this part . . .

For information on working with RubyGems, go to
www.dummies.com/extras/rubyforkids.

A-maze-ing

It's time to take the leap into graphical programs and user interfaces. Up until now, you've programmed a series of projects that used output to the terminal to interact with the code's user. ASCII art is fun, but making a project with colorful graphics that the user can interact with is even better.

In this project, you create a simple maze exploration and treasure gathering game. You can design any maze that you like using text strings that describe the level. The text looks a little like ASCII art, in fact! But in this project, your code converts it into a graphical display with different color tiles. The user moves around in the maze and collects as many treasures as she can in the least time possible.

Organizing a New Project

In this project, you'll use Atom to create and edit your program. Unlike other projects, this program's source code will be stored in five different files, one for each class you create. Each file will be named after the class it contains, and all the files will be stored in the same project directory. You'll use the terminal program to run and test the code, but this time the project will create its own window in which the game is played.

If you haven't created a development folder already, refer to Project 2 for instructions on how to do that.

1. Start your terminal program and enter the development folder:

   ```
   $ cd development
   ```

2. Create a new directory for this project:

   ```
   $ mkdir project10
   ```

3. Move in to the new directory:

   ```
   $ cd project10
   ```

4. Start Atom by double-clicking its icon.

5. Create the first source code file by choosing File ⇨ New File command. Save it by choosing File ⇨ Save and store it in your project10 directory. Call the file amazing.rb.

6. This project uses the graphical game library you installed in the first chapter (Project 1), called Gosu. If you aren't sure that you have it installed, run the following command in your terminal program:

   ```
   $ gem list
   ```

You should see a number of item lists, and a version of Gosu should be listed (see Figure 10-1). If it isn't, go back to Project 1 and follow the instructions there to install it.

Look for gosu in the list.

```
● ● ●                    project10 — bash — 80×24
Christophers-MacBook-Pro:project10 chaupt$ gem list

*** LOCAL GEMS ***

bigdecimal (1.2.0)
CFPropertyList (2.2.8)
gosu (0.9.2)
io-console (0.4.2)
json (1.7.7)
libxml-ruby (2.6.0)
minitest (4.3.2)
nokogiri (1.5.6)
psych (2.0.0)
rake (0.9.6)
rdoc (4.0.0)
sqlite3 (1.3.7)
test-unit (2.0.0.0)
Christophers-MacBook-Pro:project10 chaupt$ ▊
```

Figure 10-1: Confirm that gosu appears in your Ruby Gem list.

If some of these steps are confusing to you, refer to the "Organizing a New Project" section from Project 4. It provides more details for each step.

Get ready to search the maze for some awesome treasure!

Planning the Project

As your projects have grown, you may have noticed that the file you were writing your Ruby code in was getting a bit long. Experienced programmers who work on larger projects, alone or with teammates, usually break the code into separate files, each of which contains one specific bit of functionality. In this project, you'll start to use that technique and put (mostly) one class in each source code file.

The goal of this project is for you to create a simple, 2D game in which the player moves a piece around a mazelike board, collecting treasures and reaching the exit in the least amount of time possible. Let's figure out what objects we need for such a project:

- You need a main object that is used to setup and launch the game. This main class's job is to connect with the game library Gosu so you can use its abilities.

- You'll have another object that represents the game itself. The game object will be responsible for setting up the player object and the game board (which I'll call a *level,* although there is only one level to start). The game object will also be responsible for the player and level to display themselves, and the game object will show a user interface that displays a timer and current score.

- The level object is responsible for taking data you provide that describes what the board should look like and setting up some graphical tiles to lay out the design. The level manages movement within the maze and determines what are valid moves for the player.

- The player object is actually going to be a special version of a tile object. The tile object is an object that knows how to draw itself on the playing board. For this project, you'll have a number of different types of tiles (walls, treasure, exit, player, and so on).

To keep this project as simple as possible, I'll keep it to the objects I listed here, but as you go, you'll probably start thinking of different ways you could improve the objects you code.

What is a game engine?

The Gosu code library is a relatively simple two dimensional (2D) game engine that is great for creating many different kinds of games. But what is a game engine?

For now, think of a game engine as a collection of code that handles all the boring work needed to write a game program so you can focus on the fun stuff.

What do I mean by the boring work? Instead of having to write a lot of common code, the engine takes care of that for you. Good engines will include code for drawing graphics and text, getting input from the user, playing sound effects and music, calculating physics simulation for lifelike movement and collisions, communicating for multiple player support, and other capabilities.

A game engine typically goes through multiple steps when running your program. It first sets up the game environment, initializing the graphics support and the data needed for the game, and loading other resources that might be required (like sounds). The engine then enters what is called the *game loop*. The game loop is a loop like you've learned about, and it runs from the start of the game until the end. Inside of the loop, there are two main parts. The update part is where the engine reacts to user input and other changes to the game's data. The draw part is when all the user interface is updated and the engine draws the latest graphics based on the game data (see the following figure).

(continued)

(continued)

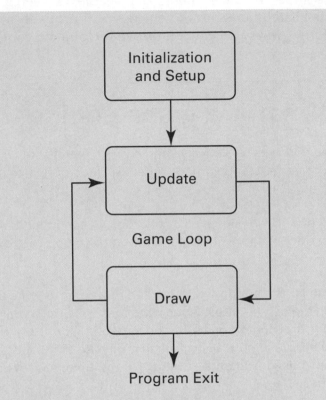

In this project, during the update part of the game loop, you'll use your keyboard's arrow keys for input to determine how to move the player. You'll also update a timer to show the player how long she has been playing.

During the draw portion of the loop, Gosu will be used to draw the maze and the pieces on it, display scores and the current elapsed time, and when the game is over, display the final Game Over message.

Looking at the Program Skeleton

This project uses a handful of classes to coordinate all the objects needed to make a simple, but very flexible game. The main starting point for your code will create all the objects needed and set up the Gosu library.

1. The `amazing.rb` source code file is your program's entry point. Add a comment to identify the file, but also write a note that helps people know how to run the program. Because there are going to be multiple files in this project, the note gives a little hint in case you forget which file is which.

```
#
# Ruby For Kids Project 10: A-maze-ing
# Programmed By: Chris Haupt
# A mazelike treasure search game
#
# To run the program, use:
# ruby amazing.rb
#
```

2. Provide a hint to Ruby as to what external code is going to be used:

```
require 'gosu'
```

Ruby doesn't automatically know about code in the other files you create or extra Ruby gems you may have loaded. The `require` line tells Ruby to look for and load `gosu` in the standard system locations.

3. Create the `Amazing` class as a child class of Gosu's `Window` class. This will connect your project up so you can use Gosu's capabilities:

```
class Amazing < Gosu::Window
def initialize
    super(640, 640)
    self.caption = "Amazing"
    # More code will go here
  end
# Even more code will go here
end
```

The class's `initialize` method creates a square window 640 pixels on a side. It also sets the window title (caption).

4. Create an instance of the class and call the Gosu `show` method to display the window and get the game going. Place this code just after the final `end` keyword:

```
window = Amazing.new
window.show
```

5. Save the code and run it in the terminal window with `$ ruby amazing.rb`. You should get a square, black window like in Figure 10-2. If not, make sure to check for any error messages in the terminal window and check for typos. If you don't have the Gosu gem installed, you may have to go back and do that.

To quit, just close the window or press Ctrl+C in the terminal.

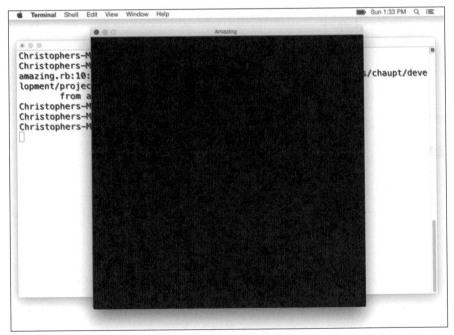

Figure 10-2: Gosu is running if you see a blank window.

Creating Placeholder Classes

There are four other classes besides the `Amazing` class you've already coded. Each of these classes will be placed in its own file and then connected using Ruby's `require` functionality.

The Game class

The Game class is responsible for setting everything up and managing all the updates and drawings that may be required from the other classes.

1. In Atom, create a new file called game.rb in the same directory as amazing.rb. Add the require functions that connect this class to others in the project:

```
require 'gosu'
require_relative 'level'
require_relative 'player'

class Game
    LEVEL1 = []
```

You've already seen the require function. The require_ relative function is used to tell Ruby to load up and use code that is in the same directory as the current file. You'll fill in the constant LEVEL1 later with your maze design.

2. Define an initialization method:

```
def initialize(window)
  @window      = window
  @player      = Player.new(@window, 0, 0)
  @level       = Level.new(@window, @player,
    LEVEL1)
  @font        = Gosu::Font.new(32)
  @time_start = Time.now.to_i
end
```

This method prepares a number of instance variables based on classes you have yet to write. The @font variable assignment looks odd — it's creating a new object using the Gosu library. Font objects are how Gosu draws text. You'll use that for some of the user interface (UI) later on. The @time_start instance variable is using Ruby's Time class to get the current time and convert it into an integer (the to_i method). That number represents the current time in seconds since the beginning of computer time!

3. Stub in the game loop related methods and end the class:

```
    def button_down(id)
    end
    def update
    end
    def draw
    end
end
```

These methods are standard functions when using Gosu. The button_down method is used to detect if the user has pressed a button on her keyboard. You'll use update to make changes to the game's data (including updating tiles based on user input). The draw method will be used to tell everything to display itself.

4. Save the code.

The Level class

The Level class is responsible for the game board and its pieces. The class will draw the maze based on a textual description you pass in.

1. In Atom, create a new file called level.rb in the same directory as amazing.rb. Add the initial Ruby require functions and class definition:

```
require 'gosu'
require_relative 'tile'
require_relative 'player'

class Level
```

2. This initialization method is a bit long, mostly because you're going to store a lot of data. I'll explain most of the variables in later sections:

```
def initialize(window, player, level_data)
  @window       = window
  @tiles        = []
  @player       = player
  @level_data   = level_data
  @total_rows   = 0
  @total_columns = 0
  @exit_reached = false
  if @level_data
    @total_rows = @level_data.length
    if @total_rows > 0
      @total_columns = @level_data.first.length
    end
    setup_level
  end
end
```

Most of the variable setup should be self-explanatory (even if you don't know what the variables are used for yet). The last part is a little complicated. It's checking to see if any level data has been supplied and, if it has, calculates the total number of rows and columns for the data before setting up the board.

The playing board for the A-maze-ing project is a grid. Think of it like a chessboard or piece of imaginary graph paper. You'll fill in each square of the grid with a wall, an empty space, or your other playing pieces (entrance, exit, treasure, and player). The layout is a little different from graphing you might have done in math class. The rows are the *y*-axis and run down vertically on your imaginary graph paper. The first row is numbered zero (0) and gets larger as you move down the paper. The columns of the grid run horizontally across the imaginary graph paper. This is your *x*-axis, and it, too, starts counting at zero (0) and increases as you move to the right. This coordinate system is how Gosu works in general (see Figure 10-3).

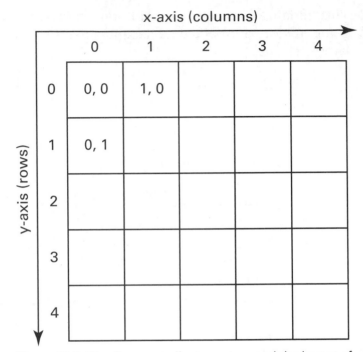

Figure 10-3: The Gosu coordinate system and the layout of a Level object's tiles.

3. Stub in the `setup_level` method for now:

```
def setup_level
end
```

4. Stub in the standard game loop methods and end the class:

```
def button_down(id)
end
def update
end
def draw
end
end
```

5. Save the code before moving on to the next placeholder.

The Tile class

The Tile class represents a visible piece on the playing board (level). It will know how to draw itself based on its type. In this project, you use a simple code to represent the type of the tile (for example, wall, empty, exit, treasure, and so on).

1. In Atom, create the tile.rb file in the same directory as the amazing.rb file. Add the require line and define the class:

    ```
    require 'gosu'

    class Tile
    ```

2. Set up a number of constants that will be used to make it a little clearer what the different types of tiles are and how big they are on screen:

    ```
    PLAYER_TYPE    = 'P'
    START_TYPE     = 'S'
    EXIT_TYPE      = 'E'
    TREASURE_TYPE  = 'T'
    EMPTY_TYPE     = '.'
    WIDTH = 32
    HEIGHT = 32
    ```

    In your level design, you'll use these symbols to place objects on a map. Any unrecognized symbol will be treated as a wall.

3. Add an attribute accessor to make it easier for other parts of the code to use a tile's variables:

    ```
    attr_reader :row, :column, :type
    ```

4. Define an initialization method for tiles:

```
def initialize(window, column, row, type)
  @@colors ||= {red: Gosu::Color.argb(0xaaff0000),
    green: Gosu::Color.argb(0xaa00ff00),
    gold: Gosu::Color.argb(0xaaffff00),
    blue: Gosu::Color.argb(0xaa0000ff)}
  @@font ||= Gosu::Font.new(24)
  @@window ||= window
  @row     = row
  @column  = column
  @type    = type
  @hidden  = false
end
```

Not only does this method set up some basic instance variables needed for any individual class (like `@row` and `@column`), but it also creates some shared class variables.

The symbol `||=` is made up of two vertical bars and one equal sign. The vertical bars are sometimes called *pipes*.

Ruby's class variables start with two at signs (`@@`) and are shared by all instances of a class. In this program, you need only one hash of colors for looking up appearance. Likewise, the font and window targeted for drawing can be shared across all tile objects. Using class variables is a convenience and saves a little memory. Perhaps the most complicated variable here is `@@colors`. The symbol `||=` means that if the variable doesn't already have a value, set it up; otherwise, don't do anything. The `@@colors` variable is being assigned a Ruby hash where the keys are names of colors, and the values are using Gosu to define a color using a hexadecimal code. You can place numbers and letters A through F in that value to change the color.

5. Stub in the draw method and finish the class:

```
def draw
  end
end
```

6. Save the code before moving on.

The Player class

The `Player` class is a specialized kind of tile object. You could break out many different special tiles, but I want to show you one that you'll use to track the user's location and score.

1. In Atom, create a `player.rb` file next to the other files in the project. Add the standard requires and class definition:

```
require 'gosu'
require_relative 'tile'

class Player < Tile
```

Because `player` is a child class of `Tile`, you'll use the subclass syntax that you've seen before.

2. Provide access to the player's score with a read-only accessor:

```
attr_reader :score
```

3. Set up the object with an initializer and close up the class with end:

```
def initialize(window, column, row)
  super(window, column, row, Tile::PLAYER_TYPE)
  @score = 0
end
end
```

Mostly this just calls its parent class using the `super` keyword. You pass the parent class the `tile` type (using the appropriate constant you set up earlier), and then set the starting score to zero.

4. Save the file before moving on. You can try running the code at this point, but you won't see anything other than a blank screen. If you get error messages in the terminal, fix those before continuing.

Coding Amazing Methods

For this project, you'll work top-down to get a feel for how the Gosu library's game loop works. The `Amazing` class kicks things off, so start there.

1. Inside of the `amazing.rb` file, add the missing `require_relative` call just below the other require:

   ```
   require_relative 'game'
   ```

2. Create a game object in the `initialize` method right after the caption is set (shown for context):

   ```
   self.caption = "Amazing"
   @game = Game.new(self)
   ```

3. Add the Gosu related game loop methods to the `Amazing` class below the `initialize` method:

   ```
   def update
     @game.update
   end

   def draw
     @game.draw
   end

   def button_down(id)
     @game.button_down(id)
   end
   ```

4. Save the file before moving on.

Coding Game Methods

The `Game` class will contain the data that describes the level and a variety of methods to help out with the game interface.

1. The `LEVEL1` constant is up first. The constant is made up of an array of 20 strings. Each string is made up of 20 characters. If you type this up in Atom and line things up, it looks like a map.

```
LEVEL1 = [
    "+-----------------+",
    "|S.|....T.........|",
    "|..|.---------..|++.|",
    "|..|.|....|T|..|T..|",
    "|.+|.|.E|.|....|...|",
    "|..|.|---.|.|--|...|",
    "|..|.|....|.|......|",
    "|+.|.|......|..|-|.|",
    "|..|.|-----.|..|+|.|",
    "|..|T.......|..|+|.|",
    "|.++--------+..|+|.|",
    "|.+....+++.....|+|.|",
    "|...++.....+++.|+|.|",
    "|---------------+..|",
    "|T+|......|.....|.||",
    "|..|..|.......+T.|.||",
    "|+...+|---------+..|",
    "|..|.............+.|",
    "|T+|..++++++++++...|",
    "+-----------------+"
]
```

The critical symbols here are the period (.) for blank spaces, S for where the player starts, E for the exit from the maze, and T for treasure markers. You can use any other symbol you like for the walls. I did a little ASCII art here using |, -, and +.

You can change this map however you like, but remember that there needs to be 20 strings of 20 characters! There also needs to be a comma at the end of each string in the array except for the last one.

2. Add code to the game loop related methods you stubbed out previously:

```ruby
def button_down(id)
  @level.button_down(id)
end

def update
  @level.update
  if !@level.level_over?
    @time_now = Time.now.to_i
  end
end
def draw
  @level.draw
  draw_hud
end
```

Mostly this just calls down to the level object to take care of things. In the update method, you'll also keep track of the current time until the player reaches the exit of the maze. You'll use the elapsed time in the heads-up display (HUD), which displays the user interface for important game information. In Amazing, the HUD will contain the current score and the clock.

3. Draw the HUD:

```ruby
def draw_hud
  if @level.level_over?
    @font.draw("GAME OVER!", 170, 150, 10, 2, 2)
    @font.draw("Collected #{@player.score}
    treasure in #{time_in_seconds} seconds!",
    110, 300, 10)
  else
    @font.draw("Time: #{time_in_seconds}", 4, 2, 10)
    @font.draw("Score: #{@player.score}", 510, 2, 10)
  end
end
```

This method changes what it draws depending on whether the level is over (the player reached the exit). If the game is still being played, the method uses Gosu's font draw method to draw text on the upper corners of the screen. If the level is over, the method displays a Game Over message and the final score.

The first three number arguments of the @font.draw method calls are the x-, y-, and z-axis locations (no, this game isn't 3D, but the z-axis is used for determining how items stack up when drawn). The other two numbers used in the Game Over message are used to scale up the size of the message. In this case, the text will be twice as high and twice as wide.

4. Add a helper for calculating the number of seconds that have gone by since the game started. Remember that you capture the current game time each pass through the Gosu game loop.

```
def time_in_seconds
  @time_now - @time_start
end
```

5. Save your code before moving on.

Coding Level Methods

The Level class is the workhorse of the game and manages all the objects needed to display the playing board.

1. Inside the level.rb file, replace the stubbed setup_level method with code that translates the string array description of the board with Tile objects:

```
def setup_level
  @level_data.each_with_index do |row_data, row|
    column = 0
    row_data.each_char do |cell_type|
      tile = Tile.new(@window, column, row,
cell_type)
```

```
          # Change behavior depending on cell_type
          if tile.is_start?
            @player.move_to(column, row)
          end
          @tiles.push(tile)
          column += 1
      end
    end
  end
```

This code uses a couple of new methods, but the concepts will be familiar. The each_with_index method is a looping method like the plain each method you've used before. Besides passing the next object to the block of code that follows, it also passes the index number of the object (its position within the array). You need to know what row number you're on, and this is a handy way to get that info.

Inside of the outer loop, you need to also track the column number (remember the graph paper metaphor I used earlier?) as you look at each row's string.

Once again, you use the each_char method of the string to loop through the characters that make up that row. Each specific character represents one of the types of tiles you want to build.

After creating the tile, you check to see if it's the starting location for the player. If it is, you get the tile's coordinates and move the player object to them.

Finally, you add the tile to the @tiles array using the array push method. Then you add one to the column count and start on the next character in the string.

2. Replace the button_down method with code that moves the player if the move is valid:

```
def button_down(id)
  if level_over?
```

```
      return
    end
    column_delta = 0
    row_delta = 0
```

First, check to see if the level is actually over. If the player reached the exit of the maze, you'll ignore any other moves since the game is done. If the level isn't over, you'll calculate the direction of the movement. Setting the variables to zero means "no movement in that direction."

3. Find out if Gosu detected any player input:

```
if id == Gosu::KbLeft
  column_delta = -1
elsif id == Gosu::KbRight
  column_delta = 1
end
if id == Gosu::KbUp
  row_delta = -1
elsif id == Gosu::KbDown
  row_delta = 1
end
```

If the player pressed one of the arrow keys on her keyboard, Gosu will pass your method an ID of that button. You use constants provided by Gosu to see which button was pressed. The numbers for the movement are based on a bit of math. If the player wants to move left, the column she wants to move to is one less than the current one, so you use −1. If the player wants to move right, it's one more (refer to Figure 10-2 if you're still uncertain about the coordinates used in the project).

The same technique is used for moving up or down a row in the maze.

Delta is a word that programmers use to mean a change in something. Here I use it to mean a change in columns or rows.

4. Now calculate whether the move is valid. You don't want the player to be able to move through walls after all! If the move is good, then move the player to the new location and get that location to see if the player reached the end of the maze or maybe found something to pick up:

```
if move_valid?(@player, column_delta, row_delta)
  @player.move_by(column_delta, row_delta)
  tile = get_tile(@player.column, @player.row)
  if tile.is_exit?
    @exit_reached = true
    tile.hide!
  else
    @player.pick_up(tile)
  end
end
```

Note that if the player moves on to the exit tile, you remember that fact in an instance variable (and hide the exit tile so it looks better).

5. Add the helper to find a tile by its coordinates:

```
def get_tile(column, row)
  if column < 0 || column >= @total_columns
    || row < 0 || row >= @total_rows
    nil
  else
    @tiles[row * @total_columns + column]
  end
end
```

The condition has logic that checks to see if the requested coordinates are outside the grid. If the request isn't correct, the method just returns nil. If the request is okay, then it calculates which tile to grab out of the @tiles array. The math is a little funky, but it's what is required to find an item in a single array that is holding a grid like yours.

6. Next, write a method to check for a valid move by the player:

```
def move_valid?(player, column_delta, row_delta)
  destination = get_tile(player.column +
    column_delta, player.row + row_delta)
  if destination && destination.
    tile_can_be_entered?
    true
  else
    false
  end
end
```

This method calculates where the player wants to move by adding her move's changes (deltas) to her current position and then using a helper method from the tile object to see if it is somewhere that can be moved into.

7. Provide a helper that can be used by other code to see if the level is done (the player reached the exit):

```
def level_over?
  @exit_reached
end
```

8. Finally, update the draw method to actually display all the tiles and the player:

```
def draw
  @tiles.each do |tile|
    tile.draw
  end
  @player.draw
end
```

9. Save your code. This class was probably the most complicated of the whole project. Take a breath before moving on!

Coding Tile Methods

The `Tile` class mostly just knows where it is located and how to draw itself. You'll provide a number of helpers to also figure out what kind of tile it is.

1. Go into the `tile.rb` file and replace the `draw` stub with the code for drawing a tile:

```
def draw
    if tile_is_drawn? && !hidden?
      x1 = @column * WIDTH
      y1 = @row * HEIGHT
      x2 = x1 + WIDTH
      y2 = y1
      x3 = x2
      y3 = y2 + HEIGHT
      x4 = x1
      y4 = y3
      c = color
      @@window.draw_quad(x1, y1, c, x2, y2, c,
x3, y3, c, x4, y4, c, 2)
      x_center = x1 + (WIDTH / 2)
      x_text = x_center - @@font.text_width
("#{@type}") / 2
      y_text = y1 + 4
      @@font.draw("#{@type}", x_text, y_text, 1)
    end
  end
```

This looks complicated, but it's almost entirely code used to draw a square with text in the middle of it. First, it checks whether it should even be drawn. There are some tiles, like the empty tile type, that should be blank. Other tiles may be hidden, so the code skips those, too.

Otherwise, the Gosu library method `draw_quad` is used to *render* (draw or display) a rectangle. You need to give it the coordinates for each corner of the shape. `x1` and `y1` are the coordinates for the upper-left corner of the square, and the rest of the variables work their way around clockwise.

The text coordinate variables try to figure out the center of the tile and draw the letter used for its type.

Watch all the punctuation on this method — there are a lot of symbols, and it's easy to make a typo. If you get errors later when testing the code, check that your code exactly matches.

2. Add a method to look up what color to draw based on the type of the tile:

```ruby
def color
  if is_player?
    @@colors[:red]
  elsif is_exit?
    @@colors[:green]
  elsif is_treasure?
    @@colors[:gold]
  else
    @@colors[:blue]
  end
end
```

This is just a big condition statement to figure out which color to pick from the @@colors class variable's hash structure.

3. Code up the methods used to move a tile:

```ruby
def move_to(column, row)
  @column = column
  @row    = row
end

def move_by(column_delta, row_delta)
  move_to(@column + column_delta, @row +
    row_delta)
end
```

The first method sets the tile's instance variables to the exact location provided. The latter method does the calculation of where the tile should move based on the delta numbers.

4. Create helper methods to test for the kind of tile:

```ruby
def is_treasure?
  @type == TREASURE_TYPE
end
def is_start?
  @type == START_TYPE
end
def is_exit?
  @type == EXIT_TYPE
end
def is_player?
  @type == PLAYER_TYPE
end
def is_empty?
  @type == EMPTY_TYPE || @type == ' '
end
```

5. Also code up some helpers to set or check whether the tile is hidden:

```ruby
def hidden?
  @hidden
end
def hide!
  @hidden = true
end
```

6. The code is going to need to make a tile empty when the player picks up an object like a treasure:

```ruby
def make_empty
  @type = EMPTY_TYPE
end
```

7. Finally, add some helpers that simplify conditions that need to test for several different common tile situations:

```
def tile_is_drawn?
  !is_empty? && !is_start?
end
def tile_can_be_entered?
  is_empty? || is_start? || is_treasure?
    || is_exit?
end
```

In many ways, these represent the "rules" of the game and how it allows movement and determines what to draw.

8. As always, save your work!

Coding Player Methods

The Player class is a special kind of tile, so it can use all the code you just wrote for tiles to display itself. Player objects also need to track a score and figure out if they can pick up another tile like a treasure.

1. Go back to the player.rb file and add the pickup functionality:

```
def pick_up(tile)
  if tile.is_treasure?
    @score += 1
    tile.make_empty
  end
end
```

If it's a treasure tile, the player's score will be updated and the old treasure tile will be cleared out.

2. That's it! Save it and test your project. If you get any errors in the terminal, go back and double-check that your code matches the instructions for writing each Ruby class above.

It's super easy to make typos. If it all works, the game should look like it does in Figure 10-4. Try moving around with the arrow keys and picking up some treasures. How fast can you collect them all and get to the green exit?

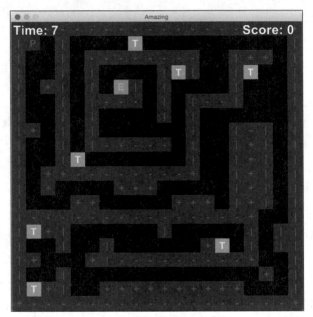

Figure 10-4: The game is alive!

Trying Some Experiments

When you get the hang of even the most basic features of Gosu, your imagination is the limit for the kinds of games and graphical programs you may create. The Ruby community has all kinds of free and open-source gems for pretty much any kind of coding need. Gosu is a great example of the kinds of code people create for the benefit of all.

There are many things you can try with the A-maze-ing code. Give a few a try:

✏ The maze for the level object is described with an array of strings. Try making your own mazes. If you want to keep them around, just define different constant names and swap in which constant you pass to the initializer.

✔ What if you wanted to add new kinds of tiles? Perhaps there are different types of treasures? Create a couple of new ones and use different colors and different numbers of points.

✔ What if there were a time limit to how long you could explore the maze? Try setting a limit, and if the time runs out, have the player lose his points.

✔ How would you make the maze window bigger and the mazes more complicated?

✔ What if the game had more than one level?

Tower

You can use computer graphics to create games, make art, study science, or understand and solve problems. Graphical programming becomes a powerful tool, and when combined with a language like Ruby, it's relatively easy to get something working with minimal work.

For the Tower project, you're going to create both a game and a tool to think about a specific algorithm. The program lets you solve the Tower of Hanoi puzzle using graphics and a point-and-click interface. If the name isn't familiar to you, you've probably seen the puzzle, where you move a stack of donutlike disks from one peg to another, without ever allowing a larger disc to sit on top of a small one.

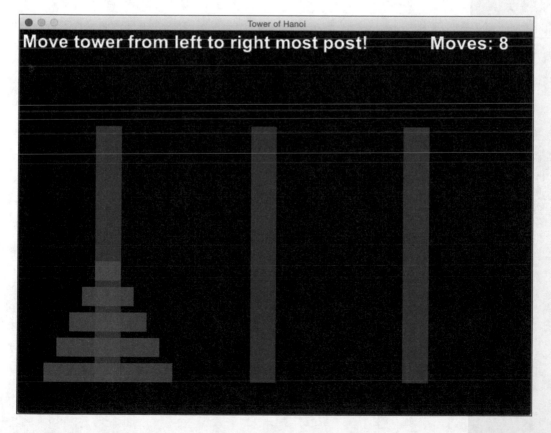

Organizing a New Project

You'll will use Atom to create and edit your program and, like the preceding project, this program's source code will be stored in multiple files, one for each class you create. Following standard Ruby practice, each file will be named after the class it contains using the lowercase version of the class name. All the files will be stored in the same project directory. The Tower project is another Gosu-based graphical program, but you'll still use the terminal program to run and test the code.

If you haven't created a development folder already, refer to Project 2 for more information on how to do that.

1. Start your terminal program and enter the development folder:

   ```
   $ cd development
   ```

2. Create a new directory for this project:

   ```
   $ mkdir project11
   ```

3. Move in to the new directory:

   ```
   $ cd project11
   ```

4. Start Atom by double-clicking its icon.

5. Create the first source code file by choosing File ⇨ New File. Save it by choosing File ⇨ Save and store it in your project11 directory. Call the file tower.rb.

6. This project uses the graphical game library called Gosu, which you installed in Project 1 and used in Project 10. If you aren't sure you have it installed, run the following command in your terminal program:

   ```
   $ gem list
   ```

You should see a number of items lists, and a version of Gosu should also be listed (refer to Figure 10-1 in Project 10).

If it isn't, go back to Project 1 and follow the instructions there to install it.

If some of these steps are confusing to you, refer to the "Organizing a New Project" section in Project 4. It provides more details for each step.

You're now ready to implement a mouse-driven interactive Tower of Hanoi puzzle game!

Planning the Project

In past projects, you learned about algorithms and how computer programs use algorithms to get work (or fun) done. In reality, algorithms are everywhere — you follow instructions and procedures all day long. Maybe you have a sequence of steps you follow when you get up in the morning, or when you do homework or work, or when you do a chore. You definitely follow steps if you play games.

The Tower of Hanoi puzzle is a math problem in disguise. What's interesting about the algorithm for this puzzle is that if you can solve the puzzle for a really easy case (one, two, or three discs), then you can also solve it for more complicated ones (lots of discs) by breaking the problem down into a series of simpler cases. Programmers have a term for this kind of approach: The solution uses a *recursive algorithm*.

The puzzle is made up of one or more discs (donuts, circles, tiles, or whatever you want to call them), each a different size. The discs sit in a stack with the largest on the bottom and the smallest on top. The pile looks a little like a pyramid. Sometimes the discs sit on posts or pegs, but that's optional. There are three positions, the starting spot with the pile of discs and two empty ones. The object is to move the entire pile from the starting pile to the last pile, one disc at a time. You can only move the topmost disc in a pile in a move, and you can never place a larger disc on top of a smaller one.

Sounds pretty easy, right?

Your program will allow the player to solve the puzzle by clicking the mouse on a graphical version of discs and pegs. The program knows the rules, so the player can't make illegal moves.

Here's what you need for the code.

- Like other projects, you'll need a main object that sets up the game and interfaces with the Gosu graphics library.

- You'll have a game object that creates all the graphical objects and knows how to manage them. The game object will also be where you create the rules of the game and the code that lets the player interact with the playing pieces.

- A post object will be the holder of zero or more discs. It will act like a container for discs and also know how to draw itself.

- The last object you need is a disc! You'll have some number of discs of different sizes. The disc objects will be fairly simple, mostly just knowing how to draw themselves when they're sitting on a post and when they're being clicked to select and move them.

It's definitely possible to come up with other collections of objects, but I'll start with this set. If you see ways to make things easier for yourself, try that out after you get the program running.

Looking at the Program Skeleton

For simple programs like this project, you can connect the main entry point of your project with the Gosu graphics library. Set up your main entry point so that it contains the required methods to work with the library and relies on your other objects to build and run the game itself.

1. Following the pattern you've been using for previous projects, the named file (`tower.rb`) will be your main starting point for

running the puzzle. Add an introductory comment to the file to kick things off:

```
#
# Ruby For Kids Project 11: Tower
# Programmed By: Chris Haupt
# Towers of Hanoi puzzle
#
# To run the program, use:
# ruby tower.rb
#
```

2. Ruby will need to be told that you're using Gosu, so do that by adding a require line. Also let the program know about the Game class you'll use for most of the functionality:

```
require 'gosu'
require_relative 'game'
```

3. Create the skeleton of the Tower class that inherits most of its behavior from Gosu's Window class:

```
class Tower < Gosu::Window

  def initialize
    super(800, 600, false)
    self.caption = "Tower of Hanoi"
    @game = Game.new(self)
  end
# More code here in a moment!
end
```

You create the game object here and pass the Tower object using the Ruby keyword self to it. Because Tower is really just a Gosu Window, by passing itself to the game, it's handing the game a window to draw and interact in.

4. At the bottom of the file, after the last `end` keyword, create an instance of the `Tower` class and display its window:

```
window = Tower.new
window.show
```

5. This code is pretty similar to the previous Gosu project. If you save and run it now, Ruby will present an error because you haven't created the `Game` class yet. Before you leave this section, stub in three more methods inside of the class, right after the `initialize` method:

```
def needs_cursor?
   true
end

def button_down(id)
   @game.button_down(id)
end

def draw
   @game.draw
end
```

There isn't much to the main Tower object — it uses the game object to do all the work. You may notice a new method called `needs_cursor?`. Its job is to tell Gosu to *not* hide the mouse pointer. Because your user will be using the mouse to click on objects in the game, you want her to be able to see where the mouse is!

Creating Placeholder Classes

In this project, you're creating three other classes that make up the behavior and appearance of the game. Each class will be in its own file, using the Ruby naming convention of the filename being the lowercase version of the class name. You'll also let Ruby know where to find the classes by using the `require` method.

The Game class

The Game class is used to connect all the other objects together, and it manages all the user interaction with those objects. This is where you'll create the code that embodies the stacking "rules" of the puzzle.

1. Using Atom, create a new file called `game.rb` in the same directory as `tower.rb`. Start out by informing Ruby what other classes and gems are going to be used:

```
require 'gosu'
require_relative 'disc'
require_relative 'post'
```

The `require_relative` method works by searching for the named item starting in the same directory as the source code file you write it in. The `require` line by itself looks in other Ruby system directories, such as where the Gosu gem was previously installed.

2. Create the `Game` class and define some useful constant variables:

```
class Game
    POST_TOP     = 150
    POST_LEFT    = 120
    POST_GAP     = 240
    POST_WIDTH   = 40
    POST_HEIGHT  = 400
    NUM_DISCS    = 5
```

Most of these variables are used to tune what the puzzle looks like. You can play with them to alter the size and shape of the other objects. You can also change the number of starting discs here.

3. Write your initialization method:

```
def initialize(window)
  @window       = window
  @font         = Gosu::Font.new(32)
  @time_start   = Time.now.to_i
  @posts        = []
  @discs        = []
  initialize_posts
  initialize_discs
  @current_disc = nil
  @move_count = 0
end
```

Because this is a Gosu program, you'll need to hang onto the window variable for use in drawing later on. You also prepare a set of arrays that hold the discs and posts for drawing and other puzzle functions.

4. Set up the posts next:

```
def initialize_posts
  0.upto(2) do |index|
    @posts << Post.new(@window,
                  POST_LEFT + (index * POST_GAP),
                  POST_TOP,
                  POST_WIDTH,
                  POST_HEIGHT)
  end
end
```

This code uses the loop methods you've seen before to create three posts. *Remember:* Programmers count starting at zero! The Post class is created with the new method, and the constants are used to tell the post what it looks like (where it is and how big it is). After the post is created, the << method adds the post to the @posts array for later use.

You'll see in a minute that there are other ways to organize and use your constants when you write the `Disc` class.

The math used in the line `POST_LEFT + (index * POST_GAP)` is just a clever way of making each post set itself up a little to the right of the last one. `POST_LEFT` is the starting place for the first post, and because the `index` value of the first post is 0, 0 times `POST_GAP` is still 0, so it stays in that place. The next post is `index` with a value of 1, so that post's position is `POST_LEFT + POST_GAP` (a little to the right). The third post is two times that distance away. A little math saves a lot of duplicate code!

5. Next, set up the discs:

```
def initialize_discs
  first_post = @posts.first
  0.upto(NUM_DISCS - 1) do |index|
    disc =  Disc.new(@window, index, first_post)
    @discs << disc
  end
end
```

You need to create multiple discs, so you again use a loop to set up each object. Discs sit on a post, so you grab the first post in the `@posts` array, and then loop through creating discs. As you'll see in a minute, discs determine their size by storing their assigned index number as a starting value, so bigger numbers represent bigger discs.

Think about how the discs are going on to the post versus how you need them to be arranged to follow the rules. It may be easier to see the bug if you draw a stack on paper to visualize this. Later on, you'll fix this problem.

6. Add a `draw` method to the class so it can display all the game objects, and close up the class with the final end keyword:

```
def draw
    @posts.each {|post| post.draw}
    @discs.each {|disc| disc.draw}
    @font.draw("Move tower from left to right most
    post!", 4, 2, 10)
    @font.draw("Moves: #{@move_count}", 640, 2,
    10)
  end
end
```

Nothing too fancy here. Each array of objects is looped through using the each method and using the short form for the following block of code (using { } instead of do and end). I added some text output so you could display some instructions and a move (click) counter.

7. Save the code before moving on. You'll add a couple of additional methods in this class later that implement the game rules and mouse support.

The Post class

The Post class manages a set of zero or more discs and gives the user a target to click on to select a destination for a disc move. As you'll see, although there appears to be a lot of code in here, almost all of it has to do with managing discs.

1. Use Atom to create a post.rb file and start the class:

```
require 'gosu'
class Post
```

First, you let Ruby know about Gosu. Then start writing the class here.

2. Set up the initialization method:

```
def initialize(window, x, y, width=40, height=400)
  @height = height
  @width  = width
  @x      = x
  @y      = y
  @color  = Gosu::Color.argb(Qxaa0000ff)
  @window = window
  @discs  = []
end
```

Most of the instance variables in this class have to do with where the post is to be displayed and what it looks like. The @discs array is dedicated to the set of discs that are sitting on the post at any given time.

One new trick is the argument list for the initialize method itself. You'll see that I included some actual values in that line, such as width=40. This is Ruby's way of suggesting a default value for a method call. In this case, if you call the new method for Post and do *not* provide a width or height in the parameter list, Ruby will fill in the parameters with the default values instead.

3. Add a draw method:

```
def draw
  @window.draw_quad(
    @x, @y, @color,
    @x + @width, @y, @color,
    @x + @width, @y + @height, @color,
    @x, @y + @height, @color)
  end
end
```

I've made the choice to have the main game object draw all of the game pieces. The draw code in the Post class only knows how to draw the post itself (as a rectangle). You could change that to have it draw its discs, too, if you want to experiment with the code later on.

4. Save the code before moving on. You'll be back to this class to finish all the disk management methods in a bit.

The Disc class

The Disc class deals with the main playing pieces for the puzzle.

1. Create the disc.rb file in Atom and fill in the start of the class:

```
require 'gosu'
class Disc
   DISC_HEIGHT       = 30
   BASE_DISC_SIZE    = 40
   DISC_VERTICAL_GAP = 10
```

You can see that there are some constant variables in the class for the disc's appearance. It's up to you where to place this information. In the Post class, you passed in the values from outside. Either is valid, so just be aware that you can do what you want.

2. Add some attribute accessor methods to make it easy to use some of the disc data outside of the disc object:

```
attr_reader     :number
attr_accessor   :post
```

Remember that attribute accessors are a shortcut for writing code to read or write values in an instance variable. attr_reader provides read-only accessors, so code outside of the disc can't change the disc's number. You'll be assigning a post to a disc later on, so the attr_accessor is used because it provides both a read access method and a write access method for you.

3. The initialization method is long, but mostly because it's setting up a lot of instance variables to draw the disc:

```
def initialize(window, number, starting_post)
  @window = window
  @number = number
  @height = DISC_HEIGHT
  @width  = BASE_DISC_SIZE * (@number + 1)
  @color  = Gosu::Color.argb(0xaaff00ff)
  @selected_color  = Gosu::Color.argb(0xaaffeeff)
  @selected = false
  @x       = 0
  @y       = 0
  @post    = starting_post
end
```

You're going to use the number of the disc as its size. The bigger the number, the larger the disc. You'll use that value to compare discs later. You can also see that the number is used to calculate the size of the disc in the @width variable by multiplying the base size by its number. Because numbers start at zero, you need to add one. (Do you know why? If you didn't add one, you'd multiply the size by zero, which is zero. A zero width would be invisible!)

4. The complicated job for a disc is to draw itself correctly. The shape is easy — it's just a rectangle. The hard part is that discs move based on where the user puts them. You'll fix up the draw method a little later after you add needed support in the Post class:

```
def draw
    @window.draw_quad(
        @x, @y, @color,
        @x + @width, @y, @color,
        @x + @width, @y + @height, @color,
        @x, @y + @height, @color)
end
end
```

5. Save your code and give it a whirl. You just have the stubs of the classes in place, so it'll look a little crazy, and you can't even click anything yet (see Figure 11-1 and Figure 11-2)!

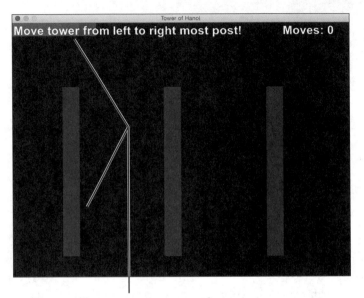

Those discs are supposed to be down there!

Figure 11-1: What's going on with those discs?

```
Christophers-MacBook-Pro:project11 chaupt$ ruby tower.rb
tower.rb:24:in `button_down': undefined method `button_down' for #<Game:0x007fb9
4186ede8> (NoMethodError)
        from tower.rb:32:in `<main>'
Christophers-MacBook-Pro:project11 chaupt$ 
```

Figure 11-2: Oops, you don't have code to handle clicks yet!

Coding Post Methods

Since the `Post` class contains most of the code needed to manage discs and is necessary to write the game rules, you should start there to finish things up.

1. First, you need some methods to allow the game to add and remove discs to the post. Add this code at the end of the Post class before the final end keyword:

```
def add_disc(disc)
  @discs.push(disc)
  disc.post = self
end

def remove_disc(disc)
  @discs.delete(disc)
  disc.post = nil
end
```

These methods use the Array class's push and delete methods, respectively. They also use the disc object's post attribute to store the current post for easy access later. When a disc is removed from a post, you're using Ruby's nil value to mean "no post."

2. Provide a little utility method to get the topmost disc on the post. In the array of discs, "top" means the last one on the array. Also create a utility to find a specific disc's position:

```
def last
  @discs.last
end
def find_disc_position(disc)
  @discs.find_index(disc)
end
```

Ruby helps you out here with the last and find_index built-in methods.

3. Remember I hinted that the discs might not be in the correct order on the post when first created? Create a method to sort things out:

```ruby
def sort_discs
  @discs.sort_by! { |disc| -disc.number }
end
```

This method uses the `Array` class's `sort_by!` method, which reorders the contents of the array in place. The block of code after that is used by Ruby to determine what attribute of the disc should be used to sort with. In this case, you want to use the number, but you want to sort in *reverse* order, so the "biggest" is at the front of the array and the smallest is at the end of the array (remember what *last* means above). To reverse things, you take the negative version of the disc's number.

4. The game is going to need some help figuring out whether a disc is being moved to a valid post. Create a method to test things out:

```ruby
def valid_move?(disc)
    disc.top_most? &&
      (@discs.empty? ||
        disc.number < last.number)
end
```

First, the code asks the disc that is about to be moved if it's on "top" of its current post (not blocked in by another disc). Then the condition code also checks that either the current post's array of discs is empty *or* if the size of the disc being moved is smaller than the topmost one on this post.

5. Provide a method to actually move the disc:

```ruby
def move_disc(disc)
  disc.post.remove_disc(disc)
  add_disc(disc)
end
```

A move happens in two steps. First, the disc removes itself from its old post; then it adds itself to the current post.

6. Now you need some methods to help with the user interface. Start with a method that determines if a click happened on the post. You'll use this fact to pick a destination for a disc.

```
def contains?(mouse_x, mouse_y)
    mouse_x >= @x && mouse_x <= @x + @width &&
    mouse_y >= @y && mouse_y <= @y + @height
end
```

Gosu provides mouse click information using X and Y coordinates. Your job is to figure out if the click is *inside* the rectangle that makes up the post's shape. This long condition compares the Xs and Ys. It can be helpful to draw a rectangle and label the four corners' coordinates if the math seems a little complicated.

7. The drawing code for discs is going to need to know where the post's position is. Provide a couple of utility methods that calculate the post's center and bottom edge:

```
def center
  @x + (@width / 2)
end

def base
  @y + @height
end
```

Remember that the Y axis goes *down instead of up* in Gosu, which is different from what you may be familiar with from beginning algebra or geometry.

8. Save all this code before moving on. You can run the program to see if you get any new errors, but the drawing and clicking problems aren't all fixed yet.

Coding Disc Methods

The `Disc` class doesn't need a lot of new code, but it does need to connect with its post and know how to draw itself.

1. Go in to the `initialize` method of the Disc class, and change the last line that starts with `@post = starting_post` to this:

   ```
   @post   = starting_post
   starting_post.add_disc(self)
   ```

   This uses the new code you just wrote in the Post class to properly add discs to the post.

2. Provide a utility method to determine if the given disc is the top one on its post:

   ```
   def top_most?
       @post.last == self
   end
   ```

   The disc's code gets its post's last disc and then compares that object's identity with itself. If the two discs are identical, then that means the disc is on top of the post. The keyword `self` in Ruby means the current object.

3. To better allow the user of the puzzle to know when she selects a disc, toggle the `@selected` variable to be `true` or `false` when the disc is clicked on:

   ```
   def toggle_selected
     @selected = !@selected
   end
   ```

   Putting the `!` symbol in front of the instance variable reverses its value. It will change `true` to `false` and `false` to `true`.

4. Just like the post, the disc needs to provide a way to detect clicks inside its rectangle:

```
def contains?(mouse_x, mouse_y)
  mouse_x >= @x && mouse_x <= @x + @width &&
    mouse_y >= @y && mouse_y <= @y + @height
end
```

5. Now you can tackle updating the draw method to properly place the disc on top of its post in the correct stack position. Replace draw with this code:

```
def draw
    if @post
        @x = @post.center - @width / 2
        position = @post.find_disc_position(self)
        if position
          if @selected
            c = @selected_color
          else
            c = @color
          end
          # calculate the y position based on
    height of post
          @y = @post.base - @height - (position *
    (@height + DISC_VERTICAL_GAP))
          @window.draw_quad(
            @x, @y, c,
            @x + @width, @y, c,
            @x + @width, @y + @height, c,
            @x, @y + @height, c)
      end
    end
  end
```

The bottom part is the same as before, almost. The top part is calculating the new X and Y positions. The X position is based on the post's center coordinate. The Y position needs to determine how high up it is from the base of the post, using its stack position to help. The long math line does that calculation for you. Lastly, you're now using two different colors when drawing discs — one color for when the disc is the active one that is clicked on and another when it isn't selected.

6. Save all this code and test things out again. It should look like Figure 11-3. Oops!

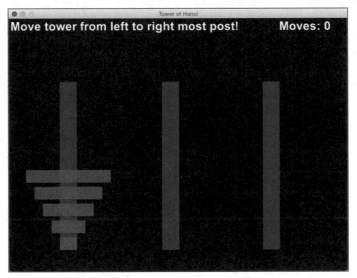

Figure 11-3: Something appears to be upside down!

Coding Game Methods

You have all the parts to fix up and run the puzzle.

1. Fix the upside-down starting tower first. Inside the Game object's initialize_discs method, add this one line right before the end keyword:

```
first_post.sort_discs
```

That will use the `sort_discs` method you wrote earlier to put the stack of discs in the proper order.

2. Write some code that will be used by the interface to manage selecting and unselecting discs. Place the method anywhere inside of the Game class:

```
def select_disc(disc)
  if @current_disc == disc
    return
  elsif @current_disc
    @current_disc.toggle_selected
  end
  @current_disc = disc
  if disc
    @current_disc.toggle_selected
  end
end
```

3. Now the "rules" of the Tower puzzle need to be created. This will have the side effect of fixing the clicking bug you keep seeing, too, since the Game object needs a `button_down` method:

```
def button_down(id)
    if id == Gosu::MsLeft
```

Gosu tells you which button was pressed. In this case, you're looking for mouse clicks using the left mouse button.

4. The game is played when the user first clicks a disc, and then clicks a target post to move the disc to. If a disc is already selected, it's being held in the `@current_disc` instance variable. In that case, check to see if a post was hit as a target:

```
if @current_disc
  hit_post = @posts.find do |post|
    post.contains?(@window.mouse_x, @window.
  mouse_y)
  end
  if hit_post && hit_post.valid_move?
    (@current_disc)
    hit_post.move_disc(@current_disc)
    select_disc(nil)
    @move_count += 1
    return
  end
end
```

First, the code looks for a post that may contain the mouse click. If a post is found, it's checked to see if a valid move is being made. If that is true, too, then the disc is moved, the selected disk is cleared out, and you keep track of the number of clicks the user has made so far.

5. Finally, handle the case when there is *not* a currently selected disc, and try to pick one:

```
hit_disc = @discs.find do |disc|
  disc.contains?(@window.mouse_x, @window.
mouse_y)
  end
  select_disc(hit_disc)
end
end
```

6. Save and run your code. The stack of discs should be in the right order, and when you click on them, they should toggle their colors. Moving them should work, too, and each successful move should update the Moves counter on the screen. See Figure 11-4 for an example.

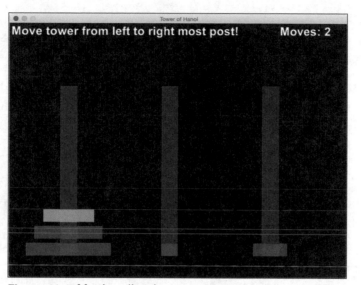

Figure 11-4: Moving discs!

Trying Some Experiments

The code in the Tower project has two jobs. First, there is all the code used to handle the interface. Gosu helps a lot here, and most of the code that seems complicated has to do with properly moving the object to be drawn to the right place on the screen. The second job of the code is to run the rules of the puzzle. This code is a lot less complicated, especially because you're able to use a lot of built-in Ruby to handle the idea of a "stack" of discs.

The code for Tower is set up so you can experiment a bit, so try some of these challenges:

✔ Change the NUM_DISCS constant variable in the Game class to 3. What is the minimum number of moves you need to make to relocate all the discs to the right side of the screen? Can you come up with a formula for this number? Test it by changing the number to 2 or 4.

✔ Alter some of the other visual elements of the game to see what happens when the size, shape, or color of a post or disc is changed.

✔ Add the ability for the user to specify the number of discs to use when the program is first run by using the `gets` Ruby method and passing the value in to the program through the various object's `initialize` methods.

A simple AI

Wouldn't it be cool if the computer could solve the puzzle for you? Here is a bonus experiment:

1. Save a copy of your program, and try the following. Open the `tower.rb` file and add the following method inside of the `Tower` class:

```
def update
  @game.update
end
```

2. Create a new file in Atom called `ai.rb`. Add this code:

```
class AI
  def move(game, num_disks, start, target, temp)
    Fiber.yield
    sleep(0.1)
    if num_disks == 1
      target.move_disc(start.last)
      game.increment_clicks
    else
      move(game, num_disks-1, start, temp, target)
      move(game, 1,                start, target, temp)
      move(game, num_disks-1, temp, target, start)
    end
  end
end
```

3. Open up `game.rb`, and add a new `require_relative` line at the top:

```
require_relative 'ai'
```

4. Add two new methods in the Game class:

```
def increment_clicks
  @move_count += 1
end
def update
  if @fiber.nil?
    @fiber = Fiber.new do
      AI.new.move(self, NUM_DISCS, @posts[0],
    @posts[2], @posts[1])
    end
  else
    @fiber.resume rescue nil
  end
end
```

5. Save your work and try running the program again. After a few seconds, it will run itself! Wow, artificial intelligence!

The explanation of how this works is a bit beyond the level of this book, but basically you're using Ruby's ability to do more than one thing at a time to calculate the next valid move. The AI class uses a technique called *recursion* to break the moves down to a simpler case. Earlier, I mention that if you can do this puzzle for one or two discs, you can do it for any number. The program does just that.

Game of Life

Have you ever wondered how a flock of birds can fly together without running into one another? What about bees building a hive or ants building a nest? When you have many animals, plants, or even software objects following simple rules all at the same time, it can lead to surprising behavior that appears quite complex.

For the last project in this book, you'll be writing the software that implements British mathematician John Conway's Game of Life. You'll use Gosu to visually explore how following a very simple set of rules can lead to cool visual effects.

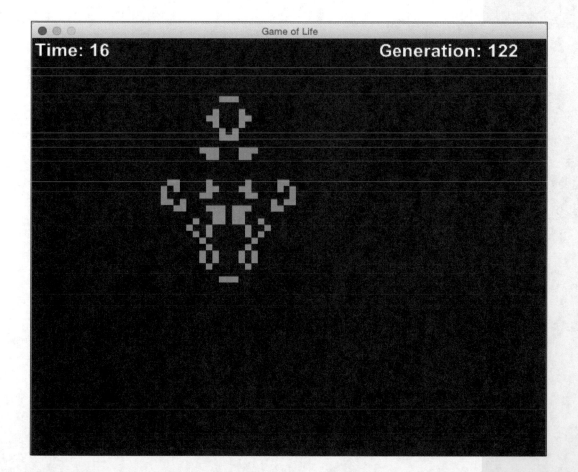

Organizing a New Project

For your last project, you'll create multiple Ruby source files using Atom. Again, all files will be named after either the project or the class that they contain, using the lowercase version of the class name when available. All the files will be stored in the same project directory. The Game of Life project uses Gosu to visualize the simulated single-cell creatures you create and also uses the command line to launch the program and gather options from the user.

If you haven't created a development folder already, refer to Project 2 for details on how to do that.

1. Start your terminal program and enter the development folder:

   ```
   $ cd development
   ```

2. Create a new directory for this project:

   ```
   $ mkdir project12
   ```

3. Move in to the new directory:

   ```
   $ cd project12
   ```

4. Start Atom by double-clicking its icon.

5. Create the first source code file by choosing File ⇨ New File. Save it by choosing File ⇨ Save and store it in your project12 directory. Call the file life.rb.

6. If you skipped to this project, make sure that you have the Gosu RubyGem installed as described in the first chapter (Project 1). If you aren't sure you have it installed, run the following command in your terminal program:

   ```
   $ gem list
   ```

You should see a number of items lists, and a version of Gosu should be listed (see Project 10 for an illustration). If it's missing, go back to Project 1 and follow the instructions there to install it.

If some of these steps are confusing to you, refer to the "Organizing a New Project" section in Project 4. It provides more details for each step.

Now you're ready to explore the fascinating world of simulation!

Planning the Project

Engineers and scientists create simulations (or sims) to explore interesting phenomena or hard-to-create experiments. Instead of having to build a spaceship and fly to the outer planets to test a theory, an expensive and possible dangerous (for the spaceship) journey, it's often possible to use math and computers to come up with a virtual experiment in software that can test some of the researcher's ideas.

In this project, you're going to study a set of rules that British mathematician John Conway invented in the 1970s. Conway called his experiment the Game of Life because it simulated the growth of a colony of single-cell creatures that followed his rules. The rules were as follows: Imagine a gridlike sheet of graph paper. On the grid, each individual box, or cell, would either be empty or occupied. For each round of the sim, you visit each cell of the grid. For each cell, you count how many neighbors the cell has. If the cell is occupied (alive), and it has two or three neighboring cells that are alive, it stays alive. If it has more or fewer neighbors, it dies. If an empty cell has exactly three neighbors, than a new cell is born in that spot. For cells on the edge of the grid, you treat all the possible neighbors that are outside of the grid as empty.

This simple set of rules leads to some fun and unexpected behavior. Scientists call this seemingly more complicated world *emergent behavior*.

You're going to recreate this experiment and get to play with it!

First, you'll need a main program that will set up the Gosu environment as in other projects. It will also gather some basic information from the user to adjust the behavior of the system. You'll use the simple command line `gets` and `puts` Ruby methods for that.

You'll create a Game class that builds and uses the other classes to run the rules of the game and display the resulting output on screen.

You're going to need a Grid class that represents your "graph paper," as described earlier. In computer programming terms, you need an array of arrays to simulate the two dimensions of the grid. In each spot you'll store your cells.

You'll need a basic object that represents the cell. Cells are alive or dead, which in turn affects how they're displayed onscreen.

This project will use some more advanced Ruby programming techniques. I'll be explaining some of them, and for others just giving some hints. ***Remember:*** The object of all of the projects is to type things in and see what happens! Don't worry if you're not clear on the programming language parts — just stay curious!

Looking at the Program Skeleton

For the Game of Life, you'll use Gosu to display the results of calculating one or more "generations" of the single-cell critters you're simulating. You'll also use regular Ruby command-line techniques to gather some input from the user before the sim is launched.

Computer scientists call software systems like the Game of Life *cellular automatons,* which is a cool name.

Begin by starting the main program code:

1. Create a `life.rb` file using Atom, and drop in an informative comment describing what the program does:

```
#
# Ruby For Kids Project 12: Life
# Programmed By: Chris Haupt
# A graphical version of Conway's Game of Life
#
# To run the program, use:
# ruby life.rb
#
```

2. Tell Ruby about the other code you'll be using with `require` method calls:

```
require 'gosu'
require_relative 'game'
```

3. Begin the `Life` class as a child class of the Gosu `Window` class so you can hook up the graphics support you'll need later:

```
class Life < Gosu::Window

  def initialize(generations, sim)
    super(800, 800)
    self.caption = "Game of Life"
    @game = Game.new(self, generations, sim)
  end
```

Notice in this project that you're passing additional parameters to the `initialize` method. You want to send some user select variable values to the game engine. One, `generations`, will be how many loops of the simulation to run, and the other will be which simulation starting environment to use (there will be many over time).

4. You'll use the `Game` class to do the actual visualization work, so pass on Gosu-related calls to that object before closing up the class:

```
def update
   @game.update
end

def draw
   @game.draw
end

end
```

5. Before creating an instance of the `Life` class, display a welcome message and gather some input from the user:

```
puts "Welcome to the Game of Life"
print "How many generations? (0 for infinite) "
generations = gets.to_i
print "Pick a simulation (1-5) "
sim = gets.to_i
```

6. Now launch the simulation by creating an instance of the `Life` class and show that object:

```
window = Life.new(generations, sim)
window.show
```

7. Save your code before moving on.

Creating Placeholder Classes

You're going to use three other Ruby classes in this project. Once again, you'll have a main game object that is responsible for the rules of the game and getting stuff displayed onscreen. The other objects will be used to store the data and assist with the calculations needed for the simulation.

The Game class

The Game class will set everything up and run the rules of the game. Start with the stubbed-out version of the class.

1. Create a new file called `game.rb` in the same directory as the `life.rb` file. Set up the require statements needed to connect all the other code:

   ```
   require 'gosu'
   require_relative 'grid'
   require_relative 'cell'
   ```

   If you don't remember the difference between `require` and `require_relative` and want to know more, see Project 11.

2. Open up the Game class and set up some initial constants:

   ```
   class Game

     GENERATION_FREQUENCY = 100 # in milliseconds
     SEED_BLINKER = [[11,10],[11,11],[11,12]]
     SEED_LIST    = [SEED_BLINKER]
     GRID_WIDTH   = 80
     GRID_HEIGHT  = 80
   ```

   The generation frequency value is how quickly the program will calculate the next set of results of the sim in milliseconds.

   Milliseconds are 1/1,000 of a second (super fast)! So 100 milliseconds is about 1/10 of a second. We want to change the simulation about 10 times a second. You can experiment with this setting to speed up or slow down the sim.

The SEED_BLINKER constant is an array of arrays. Each little array has an *x*-coordinate and a *y*-coordinate. When the system sets the simulated world up, it will use this value to populate three initial cells in the whole world. You can create your own seed patterns later and add them to the SEED_LIST.

3. Set up the initialization method:

```
def initialize(window, generations, sim)
  @window      = window
  seed         = SEED_LIST[sim - 1]
  @grid        = Grid.new(@window, GRID_WIDTH,
    GRID_HEIGHT, seed)
  @font        = Gosu::Font.new(32)
  @time_now = @time_start = Time.now.to_i
  @last_update = 0
  @generation  = 0
  @max_generations = generations.to_i
  @status_message = "Completed"
end
```

Most of the work in here is for variables used by the display of the simulation. The @grid value is the grid object, which manages our simulated world.

4. Create a utility that will be used to tell if the simulation has completed:

```
def simulation_over?
  (@max_generations > 0) && (@generation >=
    @max_generations)
end
```

You will use a comparison of the current generation and the maximum requested number of generations.

5. Create placeholder `update` and `draw` methods where you'll put the rules of the game and visual output later on. Close up the class with a final `end` keyword, too:

```
def update
end
def draw
   @grid.draw
end
end
```

6. Save your code and move on.

The Grid class

The `Grid` class will act as the container for all your cell objects, and will arrange them in a two-dimensional structure made up of an array of arrays.

1. Create a new file called `grid.rb` and enter the require statements and start of the `Grid` class:

```
require 'gosu'
require_relative 'cell'

class Grid
   include Enumerable
```

The `include Enumerable` code tells Ruby to automatically add code into this class from its `Enumerable` module. `Enumerable` provides a lot of the functionality that is used by other containers like the built-in Ruby `Array` class. You're going to make a `Grid` act just like other standard Ruby containers to simplify programming and make it more "Rubylike."

2. Set up internal variables in an initialization method:

```
def initialize(window, columns, rows, seeds=nil)
  @window        = window
  @total_rows = rows
  @total_columns = columns
  @board = setup_grid
  plant_seeds(@board, seeds)
end
```

You're using two other methods to create the grid and then set up any cells that are initially "alive."

3. The grid used in this simulation is an array of arrays. The outer array represents the rows of the grid, and each row has an array of columns. You'll sometimes refer to rows as the *y*-coordinate and the columns as the *x*-coordinate (think about graph paper if you need to).

```
def setup_grid
  grid = []
  @total_rows.times do |row|
    cells = []
    @total_columns.times do |col|
      cells << Cell.new(@window, false, col, row)
    end
    grid << cells
  end
  grid
end
```

4. The grid needs some starting values for its cells. The plant_ seeds method will either set a random collection of cells to be alive or, if a seed array is provided, use that to set cells as alive:

```
def plant_seeds(board, seeds)
  if seeds.nil? || seeds.empty?
    40.times do

      board[rand(@total_rows)][rand(@total_
      columns)].live!
    end
  else
    seeds.each do |x,y|
      cell(x,y).live!
    end
  end
end
```

The line that starts with board[rand is one long line that ends with live!. So be careful when typing that in.

5. A small utility method is used to get the cell object at a specific *x*- and *y*-coordinate in the grid. This just makes the rest of your code a little cleaner:

```
def cell(x, y)
  if @board[y]
    @board[y][x]
  else
    nil
  end
end
```

6. Finally, stub out the draw method. It won't do anything yet, but it will be ready to use some code you'll write soon to display the grid:

```
    def draw
    end
  end
```

7. Save the code and move on to the next class.

The Cell class

The Cell class's job is to store the state of the cell (alive or dead) and to display the cell based on that state.

1. Create a new file called `cell.rb` and add the standard require and start of class code:

```
require 'gosu'

class Cell
   WIDTH = 10
   HEIGHT = 10
```

You're using two constants to represent the size of the cell's square. The grid will tell it where to draw later in the initialization method.

2. Set up the starting instance variables in an initialization method:

```
def initialize(window, alive, column, row)
   @@colors ||= {red: Gosu::Color.argb(0xaaff0000),
      green: Gosu::Color.argb(0xaa00ff00),
      blue: Gosu::Color.argb(0xaa0000ff)}
   @@window ||= window
   @alive   = alive
   @column = column
   @row     = row
end
```

Note that some of the variables use the @@ symbol instead of a single @. The @@ variables are *class instance variables* and are shared across all objects that are created from this class. Why do that? Wouldn't `@window` work just as well as `@@window`? Yes, it would! However, because there are going to be a lot of `Cell` objects (80 × 80 = 6,400 of them) for each copy of the grid, and because that value for those variables will be the same, you can use this technique to save some memory and have only one of the values stored rather than lots of copies. You don't have to worry about this too much; I just wanted to show you it was possible.

3. For now, just drop in the `draw` method and close up the class:

```
def draw
  if @alive
    x1 = @column * WIDTH
    y1 = @row * HEIGHT
    x2 = x1 + WIDTH
    y2 = y1
    x3 = x2
    y3 = y2 + HEIGHT
    x4 = x1
    y4 = y3
    c = @@colors[:green]
    @@window.draw_quad(x1, y1, c, x2, y2, c,
x3, y3, c, x4, y4, c, 20)
  end
end
end
```

Here I show you a different way to set up the draw call. You're calculating each corner of the rectangle and, if the `@alive` variable is true, you're drawing the cell.

4. Save the code and test it. You haven't quite hooked things up yet, so you'll see prompts like in Figure 12-1, but then the program will crash looking for a missing method on a Cell object. Time to finish the classes up!

Input should work, but then you get an error.

```
Christophers-MacBook-Pro:project12 chaupt$ ruby life.rb
Welcome to the Game of Life
How many generations? (0 for infinite)
Pick a simulation (1-5) 1
/Users/chaupt/development/project12/grid.rb:31:in `block in plant_seeds': undefi
ned method `live!' for #<Cell:0x007fe002087e30 @alive=false, @column=11, @row=10
> (NoMethodError)
        from /Users/chaupt/development/project12/grid.rb:30:in `each'
        from /Users/chaupt/development/project12/grid.rb:30:in `plant_seeds'
        from /Users/chaupt/development/project12/grid.rb:11:in `initialize'
        from /Users/chaupt/development/project12/game.rb:14:in `new'
        from /Users/chaupt/development/project12/game.rb:14:in `initialize'
        from life.rb:16:in `new'
        from life.rb:16:in `initialize'
        from life.rb:32:in `new'
        from life.rb:32:in `<main>'
Christophers-MacBook-Pro:project12 chaupt$
```

Figure 12-1: Everything works up until the grid object is being set up.

Coding Cell Methods

The Cell class stub doesn't have a lot of additional code in it. You need to create a few methods that help make it easy to check and set its alive status.

1. Add a utility method that indicates how many life points the cell represents. For now, if the cell is alive, it's worth one point, and if it's dead it's worth zero. The game will use this to implement its rules about how many neighbors are alive. You could tweak this value to change the way the game works.

```
def life_points
    alive? ? 1 : 0
end
```

2. Instead of using Ruby accessors to work with the alive value of the object, create your own methods to check and set the state of the cell:

```
def alive?
  @alive
end
```

```
def die!
  @alive = false
end


def live!
  @alive = true
end
```

3. Because you have a nice method to check the alive status of the cell, why not clean up the draw method to use it? Change the second line of `draw` so it looks like this:

```
def draw
  if alive?
```

4. Save your code. If you test now, the error message from Figure 12-1 should be gone. Now you just see a black screen.

Coding Grid Methods

Time to put some life onto the screen! Bad pun, sorry!

1. First up, you need some methods to access the `Grid` object's contents. By adding `Enumerable` methods to the class, you allow other parts of the program to loop through the contents just like any other built-in Ruby container. Start with an `each` method:

```
def each
  @total_rows.times do |row|
    @total_columns.times do |col|
      yield cell(col, row)
    end
  end
end
```

This code uses the Ruby `yield` statement, which passes its parameter to another block of code. This fills in the variables you see between the vertical bar characters (| |) when you use the `each` method on arrays and other containers. Here, you're looping through each column of each row, one cell at a time.

2. Although the `each` method returns each cell, you also want to sometimes loop over the whole grid and get the *x*- and *y*-coordinates of each of those cells instead:

```
def each_cell_position
  @total_rows.times do |row|
    @total_columns.times do |col|
      yield col, row
    end
  end
end
```

3. You can use the above methods to determine if there is any life on the entire grid. This check will be useful for implementing the game rules later on:

```
def lifeless?
  none? do |cell|
    cell.alive?
  end
end
```

The `none?` method comes from the Ruby `Enumerable` module that you included earlier and uses the `each` method you created to test each cell to make sure that *none* of them is true (alive).

4. You also want the opposite kind of check so you can collect all cell positions that are alive. You'll use that later to act as a seed creating future generations of the grid.

```
def life
  living_cells = []
  each_cell_position do |x,y|
    living_cells << [x,y] if cell(x,y).alive?
  end
  living_cells
end
```

5. A slightly more complicated piece of code is the method that checks each of the surrounding cells from the current one to see how many of the neighbors are alive:

```
def surrounding_cells(x, y)
  cells = []
  (y - 1).upto(y + 1) do |row|
    (x - 1).upto(x + 1) do |column|
      next if row < 0 || row >= @total_rows
      next if column < 0 || column >=
      @total_columns
      next if x == column && y == row
      cells << cell(column,row)
    end
  end
  cells.compact
end
```

This looks complicated, but once you understand the syntax, it isn't too bad.

It sets up two loops:

• The outer loop looks at each row starting one above the current row and ending one below the current row.

• A second loop looks at the columns just to the left of the current column and ends on the column immediately to the right of the current column.

If you think about graph paper again, you can imagine that there are eight squares that surround any single non-edge square.

The three `next` statements check to make sure that the row and columns don't fall outside of the grid. If they do, they're automatically considered "empty" cells. You also want to ignore the cell itself, because it can't be a neighbor of itself.

Finally, you collect the remaining cells into a `cells` array. Some of those cells may be `nil` because of possible programming mistakes. The `compact` method of the `Array` class cleans out any `nil` values from an array, leaving just real cells behind.

6. You need a method that allows one grid to be compared with another one. One of the rules you'll create shortly says that if the grid doesn't change from generation to generation, it's considered "frozen," and the sim should end. Here you're comparing the two grids' lists of "live" cells to see if they're identical:

```
def ==(other)
  self.life == other.life
end
```

This method looks a little strange, but it shows you that you can use symbols like == for the name of a method just as easily as letters and numbers.

7. Finally, update the `draw` method to use the earlier code to walk through each cell and have it display itself:

```
def draw
  each do |grid_cell|
    if grid_cell
      grid_cell.draw
    end
  end
end
```

8. Save your code and test again. You shouldn't get any errors, and you start to see some (simple) life on the screen (see Figure 12-2).

That's a blinker between blinks!

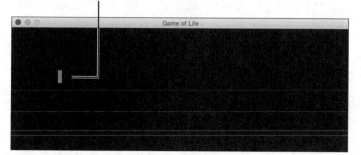

Figure 12-2: This little critter is just waiting to dance.

Coding Game Methods

You have all the parts you need to actually implement Conway's Game of Life rules and get a user interface up on the screen.

Programming the user interface

The simulation will be interesting to look at, but it will be even better if you provide some feedback to the user regarding what is happening:

1. Starting with the user interface, update the draw method to also display a generation counter and timer:

```
def draw
  @grid.draw
  draw_hud
end
```

2. The heads-up display (HUD) uses Gosu text drawing code like you used in earlier projects:

```
def draw_hud
  if simulation_over?
    @font.draw("Sim all done!", 200, 150, 10, 2, 2)
    @font.draw("#{@status_message} in #
    {@generation} generations after #{time_in_
    seconds} seconds!",
     110, 300, 10)
  else
    @font.draw("Time: #{time_in_seconds}",
     4, 2, 10)
    @font.draw("Generation: #{@generation}",
     540, 2, 10)
  end
end
```

While the simulation is running, it will show the time and generation counter. If the sim completes for any reason, the HUD will show the final message and generation count.

3. Create the small utility method that the HUD needs to calculate the elapsed time:

```
def time_in_seconds
  @time_now - @time_start
end
```

Writing the game rules

The Game of Life rules are run in a loop, where the code examines the grid and all the cells on it, determines which cells change, and then creates a new grid with the results. This loop will continue until the maximum generations are reached or the game is in a state that can't progress further. The two cases you'll look for are if the grid is empty of life or if the grid isn't changing from generation to generation.

1. Start by replacing the Game class update method and determining the current time:

```
def update
  this_time = Gosu::milliseconds()
```

Gosu provides a method that calculates the number of milliseconds since the game started. You'll use that to determine if enough time has passed before calculating a new generation of cells.

Gosu runs its game loop at a speed that tries to be as close to the requested frame rate as possible. The *frame rate* is the number of times per second that the program tries to refresh the screen. The word *frame* refers to a screen's worth of data. By default, this is set to be 60 frame (screen) updates a second. If you calculated a new generation each time update was called at this rate, the simulation would run too quickly. For this project, you want to update the simulation only 10 times a second, so you need to write some code to wait until the right amount of time has passed.

2. Check that the right amount of time has passed:

```
if (this_time - @last_update > GENERATION_
    FREQUENCY &&
  (@max_generations == 0 ||
  @generation < @max_generations))
  new_grid = evolve
  @generation += 1
```

The condition checks a couple of things. First, has the desired amount of time passed? Second, does the simulation have no limit on number of generations or, if it does, has that limit not yet been reached? If the condition passes, then you'll calculate a new grid with the evolve method and increase the generation counter.

3. Now check the new grid to see if it's still viable (able to support new generations):

```ruby
if new_grid.lifeless?
  @status_message = "Life disappeared"
  @max_generations = @generation
elsif new_grid == @grid
  @status_message = "Life froze"
  @max_generations = @generation
end
```

This set of conditions uses the methods you wrote in the Grid class to test the board for lack of life or a board that isn't changing. You use a little trick of setting the @max_generations instance variable to the current generation as a way of making the condition at the top of the update method fail so you no longer run the simulation. If the grid is stuck for some reason, there is no point in continuing.

4. Finish the update method with some variable updates:

```ruby
    @grid = new_grid
    @last_update = this_time
    @time_now = Time.now.to_i

  end
end
```

Swap out the old grid with the new one and keep track of the time for the next pass.

5. The evolve method's job is to walk through the entire current grid and apply the Game of Life rules to each cell. You then create a new grid using those cells as the seed cells for another round:

```
def evolve
  life = []
  @grid.each_cell_position do |x,y|
    if determine_fate(x, y)
      life << [x, y]
    end
  end
  Grid.new(@window, GRID_WIDTH, GRID_HEIGHT, life)
end
```

6. The rules of the game are in the `determine_fate` method:

```
def determine_fate(x, y)
    cell = @grid.cell(x, y)
    neighbors = @grid.surrounding_cells(x, y)
    score = 0
    neighbors.each {|n| score += n.life_points}
    (cell.alive? && score >= 2 && score <= 3) ||
    (score == 3)
  end
```

For the coordinates that are passed in as parameters, you get the cell, find all the cell's neighbors, and count how many are alive. Remember that the rules say that if the current cell is alive, then it needs to have a neighbor score of 2 or 3 to stay alive. If the current cell is not alive, then it is "born" if the neighbor score is 3 only. For all other conditions, the cell "dies."

7. Save the code and try running it now. It should start animating. If you set a number of generations to run, it should stop after that number (check out the HUD!) and look like Figure 12-3. The seed pattern you have in the code now is called the "blinker" pattern. Why is that?

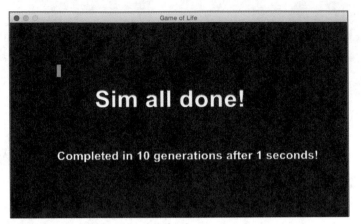

Figure 12-3: Blinker has blinked.

Adding more seed patterns

The fun thing about this project is that there are a lot of different patterns to experiment with. You'll add a few more here to get started.

1. Inside of the Game class, add the following constants immediately under the SEED_BLINKER line:

```
SEED_RANDOM  = []
SEED_GLIDER  = [[1,0],[2,1],[0,2],[1,2],[2,2]]
SEED_THUNDER = [[30,19],[30,20],[30,21],[29,17],
    [30,17],[31,17]]
SEED_GROWER  = [[12,12],[13,12],[14,12],[16,12],
    [12,13],[15,14],[16,14],[13,15],[14,15],[16,15],
    [12,16],[14,16],[16,16]]
```

Watch the use of square brackets and commas when typing this in. It's easy to make a typo here.

2. Update the SEED_LIST array with the names of the new constants:

```
SEED_LIST    = [SEED_RANDOM, SEED_BLINKER, SEED_
    GLIDER, SEED_THUNDER, SEED_GROWER]
```

3. Save the code and run it again. This time, as you type different numbers for the "Pick a simulation (1–5)" prompt, you should see different results (see Figure 12-4 for one possible example). How would you describe each pattern you see?

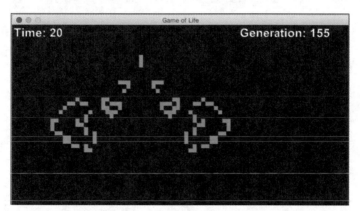

Figure 12-4: Some sims generate interesting patterns after some time.

Trying Some Experiments

The Game of Life opens up all kinds of interesting experiments you could try, just by changing the seed patterns. Because it's such a widely studied algorithm, you can find lots of suggestions online — some that create repeating patterns, some that freeze after a time, and some that generate new patterns forever.

- Try creating a few of your own lists of coordinates in the Game class and add them to the SEED_LIST. Can you make ones that fill the screen?

- Change the number of seed cells that are created for the random option in the plant_seeds method of the Grid class. What happens with bigger or smaller numbers?

- Using what you learned in the previous project, add support for clicking the mouse on the grid and have that create a new live cell in that spot. This one is hard, but can lead to lots of interesting discoveries.

✔ Look up Conway's Game of Life online and find some of the repeating patterns and different "life forms" that are out there. Can you re-create some of them in this program? The Wikipedia page (`https://en.wikipedia.org/wiki/Conway%27s_Game_of_Life`) is a good place to start to see some "still lifes," "oscillators," and "spaceships" among others. Just convert the graph-paper-like locations into x- and y-coordinates and enter them into an array like the other seed patterns in this project.

Index

Notes

Notes

Notes

Notes

Notes

Notes

About the Author

Christopher Haupt is a computer scientist, entrepreneur, game designer, and startup advisor who loves to spend his time teaching and mentoring kids of all ages on the wonders of programming. Christopher is an active member within his regional school district and broader community, helping to grow interest and support for STEAM programs, science fairs, and other places kids can explore technology, exercise their curiosity, and release their creativity.

Dedication

This book is dedicated to my kids, Zachary and Sydney Haupt. The two of you continue to inspire me to find new ways to help the next generation of scientists, technologists, engineers, artists, and mathematicians grow and be successful.

Author's Acknowledgments

I'd like to give special thanks to everyone who advised me and helped with testing each of the projects and making suggestions, including Sydney Haupt, Lynda Haupt, the fine folks of the Sacramento Ruby (#SacRuby) Meetup and Sacramento HackerLab, Don Scott and all of his great students over the years at EV Cain STEM Charter Middle School, and my technical reviewers. I also deeply appreciate the support of the following: Carole Jelen, for getting me writing professionally again; Elizabeth Kuball, for making what I write intelligible; my readers and local students, family, and friends; all of my social media followers; and the awesome team at Wiley. All the good stuff is due to the help of these wonderful people. All the typos and mistakes are my own!

Publisher's Acknowledgments

Executive Editor: Steve Hayes

Project Editor: Elizabeth Kuball

Copy Editor: Elizabeth Kuball

Technical Editor: Srinivas Kolli

Production Editor: Kinson Raja

Apple & Mac

iPad For Dummies,
6th Edition
978-1-118-72306-7

iPhone For Dummies,
7th Edition
978-1-118-69083-3

Macs All-in-One
For Dummies, 4th Edition
978-1-118-82210-4

OS X Mavericks
For Dummies
978-1-118-69188-5

Blogging & Social Media

Facebook For Dummies,
5th Edition
978-1-118-63312-0

Social Media Engagement
For Dummies
978-1-118-53019-1

WordPress For Dummies,
6th Edition
978-1-118-79161-5

Business

Stock Investing
For Dummies, 4th Edition
978-1-118-37678-2

Investing For Dummies,
6th Edition
978-0-470-90545-6

Personal Finance

Personal Finance
For Dummies, 7th Edition
978-1-118-11785-9

QuickBooks 2014
For Dummies
978-1-118-72005-9

Small Business Marketing
Kit For Dummies,
3rd Edition
978-1-118-31183-7

Careers

Job Interviews
For Dummies, 4th Edition
978-1-118-11290-8

Job Searching with Social
Media For Dummies,
2nd Edition
978-1-118-67856-5

Personal Branding
For Dummies
978-1-118-11792-7

Resumes For Dummies,
6th Edition
978-0-470-87361-8

Starting an Etsy Business
For Dummies, 2nd Edition
978-1-118-59024-9

Diet & Nutrition

Belly Fat Diet For Dummies
978-1-118-34585-6

Mediterranean Diet
For Dummies
978-1-118-71525-3

Nutrition For Dummies,
5th Edition
978-0-470-93231-5

Digital Photography

Digital SLR Photography
All-in-One For Dummies,
2nd Edition
978-1-118-59082-9

Digital SLR Video &
Filmmaking For Dummies
978-1-118-36598-4

Photoshop Elements 12
For Dummies
978-1-118-72714-0

Gardening

Herb Gardening
For Dummies, 2nd Edition
978-0-470-61778-6

Gardening with Free-Range
Chickens For Dummies
978-1-118-54754-0

Health

Boosting Your Immunity
For Dummies
978-1-118-40200-9

Diabetes For Dummies,
4th Edition
978-1-118-29447-5

Living Paleo For Dummies
978-1-118-29405-5

Big Data

Big Data For Dummies
978-1-118-50422-2

Data Visualization
For Dummies
978-1-118-50289-1

Hadoop For Dummies
978-1-118-60755-8

Language & Foreign Language

500 Spanish Verbs
For Dummies
978-1-118-02382-2

English Grammar
For Dummies, 2nd Edition
978-0-470-54664-2

French All-in-One
For Dummies
978-1-118-22815-9

German Essentials
For Dummies
978-1-118-18422-6

Italian For Dummies,
2nd Edition
978-1-118-00465-4

Available in print and e-book formats.

Available wherever books are sold. **For more information or to order direct visit www.dummies.com**

Math & Science

Algebra I For Dummies,
2nd Edition
978-0-470-55964-2

Anatomy and Physiology
For Dummies, 2nd Edition
978-0-470-92326-9

Astronomy For Dummies,
3rd Edition
978-1-118-37697-3

Biology For Dummies,
2nd Edition
978-0-470-59875-7

Chemistry For Dummies,
2nd Edition
978-1-118-00730-3

1001 Algebra II Practice
Problems For Dummies
978-1-118-44662-1

Microsoft Office

Excel 2013 For Dummies
978-1-118-51012-4

Office 2013 All-in-One
For Dummies
978-1-118-51636-2

PowerPoint 2013
For Dummies
978-1-118-50253-2

Word 2013 For Dummies
978-1-118-49123-2

Music

Blues Harmonica
For Dummies
978-1-118-25269-7

Guitar For Dummies,
3rd Edition
978-1-118-11554-1

iPod & iTunes
For Dummies, 10th Edition
978-1-118-50864-0

Programming

Beginning Programming
with C For Dummies
978-1-118-73763-7

Excel VBA Programming
For Dummies, 3rd Edition
978-1-118-49037-2

Java For Dummies,
6th Edition
978-1-118-40780-6

Religion & Inspiration

The Bible For Dummies
978-0-7645-5296-0

Buddhism For Dummies,
2nd Edition
978-1-118-02379-2

Catholicism For Dummies,
2nd Edition
978-1-118-07778-8

Self-Help & Relationships

Beating Sugar Addiction
For Dummies
978-1-118-54645-1

Meditation For Dummies,
3rd Edition
978-1-118-29144-3

Seniors

Laptops For Seniors
For Dummies, 3rd Edition
978-1-118-71105-7

Computers For Seniors
For Dummies, 3rd Edition
978-1-118-11553-4

iPad For Seniors
For Dummies, 6th Edition
978-1-118-72826-0

Social Security
For Dummies
978-1-118-20573-0

Smartphones & Tablets

Android Phones
For Dummies, 2nd Edition
978-1-118-72030-1

Nexus Tablets
For Dummies
978-1-118-77243-0

Samsung Galaxy S 4
For Dummies
978-1-118-64222-1

Samsung Galaxy Tabs
For Dummies
978-1-118-77294-2

Test Prep

ACT For Dummies,
5th Edition
978-1-118-01259-8

ASVAB For Dummies,
3rd Edition
978-0-470-63760-9

GRE For Dummies,
7th Edition
978-0-470-88921-3

Officer Candidate Tests
For Dummies
978-0-470-59876-4

Physician's Assistant Exam
For Dummies
978-1-118-11556-5

Series 7 Exam For Dummies
978-0-470-09932-2

Windows 8

Windows 8.1 All-in-One
For Dummies
978-1-118-82087-2

Windows 8.1 For Dummies
978-1-118-82121-3

Windows 8.1 For Dummies,
Book + DVD Bundle
978-1-118-82107-7

Available in print and e-book formats.

Available wherever books are sold. **For more information or to order direct visit www.dummies.com**

Take Dummies with you everywhere you go!

Whether you are excited about e-books, want more from the web, must have your mobile apps, or are swept up in social media, Dummies makes everything easier.

Leverage the Power

For Dummies is the global leader in the reference category and one of the most trusted and highly regarded brands in the world. No longer just focused on books, customers now have access to the For Dummies content they need in the format they want. Let us help you develop a solution that will fit your brand and help you connect with your customers.

Advertising & Sponsorships

Connect with an engaged audience on a powerful multimedia site, and position your message alongside expert how-to content.

Targeted ads • Video • Email marketing • Microsites • Sweepstakes sponsorship

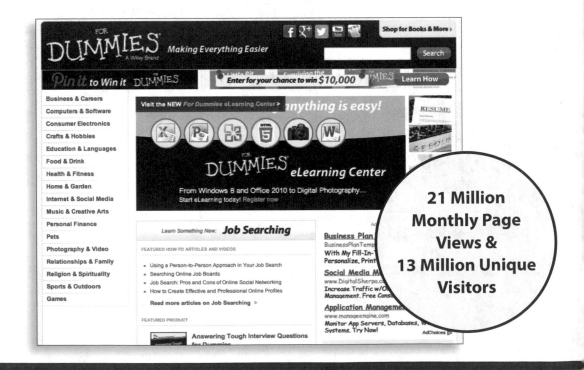